Project Management Essentials: Strategies for Success

SRINATH KOTA

DEDICATION

To my wife, Kalpana
Thank you for being my muse, my confidant, and my partner in every adventure. This book is as much yours as it is mine, for you are the heart and soul that breathe life into these word.

TABLE OF CONTENT

CHAPTER 1 Project Initiation..1

CHAPTER 2 Planning and Scheduling..15

CHAPTER 3 Risk Mangement..29

CHAPTER 4 Team Leadership and Communication 41

CHAPTER 5 Budgeting and Cost Control......................................49

CHAPTER 6 Quality Assurance and Control.................................58

CHAPTER 7 Change Management 67

CHAPTER 8 Execution and Monitoring 74

CHAPTER 9 Project Closure 86

CHAPTER 10 Emerging Trends in Project Management............96

CONCLUSION..106

REAL TIME EXAMPLES 109
TIPS FOR EFFECTIVE PROJECT MANAGEMENT 112

ACKNOWLEDGMENTS

I want to express my profound gratitude to my family. Your understanding and patience have been my constant pillars of support throughout this creative journey. Your belief in me and your willingness to give me the time and space to write have been invaluable.

CHAPTER 1
PROJECT INITIATION

PROJECT MANAGEMENT

For many individuals who are not familiar with the business world, the term 'project management' can activate a range of thoughts, leaving them unable to narrow down their stream of thoughts, and so, arrive at a clear and definitive understanding of what it entails and why it's essential. Before delving into the technical aspects of project management, it's crucial to have a complete understanding of what constitutes a project and how it corelates to the concept of project management.

A project – in its simplest form is an organized and time-bound effort meant to achieve a specific *objective*, typically with well-defined parameters from its start to end. The end goal, however, is always focused on delivering a set and defined *outcome* or *product*.

Although human beings have been born as solution-driven creatures, as the concept goes for many individuals, that the creator placed them on this Earth to engage in innovations, create the unknown, and solve the most complicated of issues to make life easier for themselves. Yet, it wasn't until the mid-20th century that project management emerged as a recognized management discipline. This development was largely necessitated by the due to the increasing complexity of modern projects, involving large infrastructure construction leading to intricate processes, diverse stakeholders, advanced technologies, and space exploration.

Ranging across various industries and organizations, project management is significantly put into use for streamlining processes, ensuring that both large-scale initiatives and routine operational tasks are completed efficiently and effectively. Although primarily associated with projects like introducing innovative products or embarking on digital transformations, with its need to adopt new trends and environmental needs, the niche has expanded itself, especially among larger organizations, to enhance the efficiency of routine operations, and so, deliver greater value.

ITS ROLE IN THE CURRENT BUSINESS LANDSCAPE

Crucially, project management is indispensable for organizations aiming to create, revamp, or launch products or services. Even on an intimate level, individuals can use project management principles to handle personal tasks efficiently. Every project, regardless of its scale, revolves around three core components: duration, quality, and resource management. The Project Manager, equipped with the necessary skills, takes charge of planning, execution, and delivery.

At the core of project management are *five* key stages: **Initiation**, **Planning**, **Execution**, **Monitoring**, and **Closing**. While these stages are conceptually broad, a competent and skillful project manager will be able to personalize and improvise these steps to suit a specific project at hand. The implementation of these steps can vary based on the type of project management methodology employed.

Any designated project manager must define a project's scope, adhering to the established budget, managing human resources, meticulously documenting each step, addressing challenges, and conducting quality checks before project delivery. Project management, with its structured approach and skilled Project Managers, is indeed the need of the day to navigate the complexities of modern projects and drive successful outcomes in today's dynamic business environment.

Effective management is essential to coordinate these elements and ensure successful outcomes. Project management optimizes resource allocation, encompassing time, money, and personnel, preventing wastage. It offers tools and techniques for risk identification, assessment, and mitigation, addressing inherent project risks such as budget overruns and unexpected obstacles. Project management establishes clear roles and responsibilities, developing a sense of ownership and accountability among team members and stakeholders. In a nutshell, comprehensive project documentation facilitates transparency and knowledge transfer throughout the project lifecycle.

SIGNIFICANCE OF PROJECT INITIATION

The significance of **Project Initiation** cannot be overstated in the realm of effective project management. It forms the foundation upon which successful projects are erected. During this phase, the raw idea based on which the project came into existence, is methodically *defined*, *evaluated*, and *ratified* for further procedures. This process involves carefully documenting all substantial evidence and proofs to justify the project and its happenings in the near future, deciding what the major significant deliverables will be and within what time frame must they all be completed, estimating, and analyzing potential risks, calculating estimated costs, listing and finding sources for resource requirements, and discussing all other essential project details.

The Initiation Phase represents a structured approach to project initiation, offering a multitude of benefits. It guides the project team in clarifying and articulating key aspects of the proposed project, aiding decision-making processes. Moreover, it ensures that the projects chosen to move forward are poised for success. The effort invested in this phase varies with the project's size and complexity, ranging from hours for smaller operational projects to weeks for large strategic endeavors. However, regardless of project size, maintaining a laser focus on the Initiation Phase's purpose is paramount: producing a Project Charter that authorizes the project's progression and serves as the cornerstone for all subsequent project management and planning activities. In essence, project initiation sets the stage for a project's entire lifecycle, providing the clarity and direction needed for a successful journey from concept to completion.

PROJECT CHARTER

The ultimate output of this phase, the **Project Charter**, plays a pivotal role in ensuring the success of technology projects. A well-crafted Project Charter serves as a guiding document, facilitating a common understanding among all project stakeholders regarding the project's objectives, expected benefits, technical approach, and how its deliverables will integrate into ongoing operations.

Creating a project charter is the foundational step in the project management process. It begins with a clear and descriptive project overview, which includes a project title that succinctly conveys the project's primary goal. The project overview also encompasses a concise description of the project's purpose, priority level, major goals, milestones, and dependencies on previous or concurrent projects. It's essential to specify the project management methodologies to be employed, such as Agile, Kanban, or Scrum. Additionally, this phase involves outlining how task status, documentation, result delivery, system deployment rules, teamwork methodologies, and meetings will be managed. Links to project dashboards and team portals are included for easy access to real-time project status updates.

Identifying stakeholders and their interests is a critical aspect of the project charter. This section lists all stakeholders along with their roles and responsibilities. A clear definition of goals, roles, and responsibilities helps eliminate confusion within the project team and among management. It's also advisable to establish a communication plan, ensuring that preferred contact frequency and communication styles are established early in the project.

Conducting an initial risk assessment is another vital component. This section of the project charter should describe potential risks that the project may encounter. Risk assessment is crucial for anticipating challenges and addressing them proactively before they escalate and cause delays or budget overruns. To align the project with organizational goals, it's imperative to define success criteria, which can include ROI projections, sales increases, issue resolutions, or other relevant factors depending on the project type. Without these terms for success, it becomes challenging to ensure the project contributes to the organization's continuous improvement.

Lastly, the project charter should outline an estimated project schedule that realistically reflects the time required for task completion. Involving the project team and stakeholders in this process is essential to gather input and ensure accuracy. The schedule should account for unforeseen emergencies to prevent project derailment.

In essence, the project charter serves as the project's roadmap, beginning with a clear overview, followed by stakeholder identification, risk assessment, alignment with organizational goals, and a realistic project schedule. This comprehensive document sets the stage for successful project management by providing a shared understanding of project objectives and expectations from the outset.

THE NEED TO IDENTIFY STAKEHOLDERS & THEIR INTERESTS

When it comes to a project, stakeholders needs to be understood as an umbrella term for a diverse group of individuals and entities, including **customers, employees, community members, politicians, media, shareholders, suppliers, investors, government departments, regulators, neighboring businesses,** and **nearby residents**. These stakeholders, along with their extended networks of family, friends, and colleagues, share several traits. They each have their own goals and objectives, often influenced by their unique interests and roles. Additionally, they possess the authority or influence to make decisions that can significantly affect your organization, whether through direct actions or advocacy. The decisions made by your organization can have a tangible impact on the lives and well-being of these stakeholders, and these changes can result in financial or physical consequences, being both positive as well as negative. Moreover, these stakeholders are part of broader networks of people, extending their influence and the ripple effects of organizational decisions to a wider community.

Businesses frequently consider the interests and concerns of their stakeholders when making significant changes, introducing new initiatives, or discontinuing existing ones, to ensure that all these decisions meet the expectations of all those involved. By considering the perspectives and interests of stakeholders, businesses aim to make informed choices that not only benefit the organization but also take into consideration the potential impacts and implications on customers, employees, shareholders, local communities, regulatory bodies, suppliers, and other parties who have a vested interest in the business. This approach ensures greater transparency, accountability, and alignment between the organization and its stakeholders, ultimately contributing to more successful and sustainable business practices.

Identifying stakeholder interests is imperative for a couple of reasons. Firstly, it allows businesses to **incorporate diverse perspectives** into their decision-making processes. When multiple stakeholder interests considered, it **broadens the scope of considerations** and helps ensure that decisions are well-rounded and balanced. Let's consider, a city is embarking on a major infrastructure project to build a new highway system. In addition to the interests of government departments and politicians, they must consider the concerns of residents and neighboring businesses because neglecting their interests could lead to negative consequences such as legal disputes, delays, or community protests. By engaging with residents and businesses, the city can find solutions that minimize disruptions, address environmental concerns, and ultimately lead to a smoother project implementation that benefits everyone. While it may not always be possible to please every stakeholder, considering a variety of perspectives increases the likelihood of making choices that benefit a broader spectrum of people.

Secondly, recognizing and accommodating stakeholder interests can lead to **greater support for business initiatives**. When stakeholders feel that their concerns and priorities are taken into consideration, they are more likely to support the business and organization's endeavors. Imagine a technology company planning to launch a groundbreaking new product. While their investors are primarily interested in maximizing returns, the company must also consider the interests of their customers and employees. Focusing solely on investor interests might lead to aggressive cost-cutting, potentially compromising product quality and employee morale. By acknowledging the interests of customers and employees, they can strike a balance, ensuring a high-quality product and a motivated workforce, which ultimately contributes to higher customer satisfaction and long-term profitability. In essence, stakeholder support can **facilitate smoother operations and garner goodwill** from various quarters.

Furthermore, considering stakeholder interests **helps improve the overall success rate of business decisions**. Put this into perspective now - a retail chain plans to expand its operations by opening new stores. While shareholders may focus on maximizing profits, the company should also weigh the interests of its employees and customers. If they prioritize only financial gains and cut costs excessively, it could result in understaffed stores, reduced customer service quality, and employee dissatisfaction. By recognizing the importance of employees and customers, the company can ensure a positive shopping experience, employee retention, and sustained customer loyalty, which in turn drives long-term profitability. Therefore, identifying and balancing stakeholder interests is essential to minimize risks and enhance the chances of successful outcomes for business initiatives.

CONDUCTING INITIAL RISK ASSESSMENT

With respect to project management, a "risk assessment" is a systematic and structured process used to evaluate and analyze potential risks that may impact a project's *objectives*, *timelines*, *budget*, and *overall success*. Risk assessment aims to provide project managers and their teams with a proactive approach to understanding and moderating potential challenges, allowing them the time and space for informed decision-making and risk mitigation strategies. It involves a few key components as discussed in detail below:

1. **Identification**: The first step involves identifying all possible risks that could affect the project. This can encompass a wide range of factors, including technical, financial, logistical, and external variables.

2. **Categorization**: Once identified, risks are categorized based on their nature and impact. Common risk categories may include technical risks, operational risks, financial risks, or external risks related to market changes or regulatory shifts.

3. **Prioritization**: Risks are then prioritized based on their probability of occurrence and potential impact. High-impact, high-probability risks typically receive the most attention and resources for mitigation planning.

4. **Qualitative Assessment**: Risk assessments often use qualitative measures, considering factors like the likelihood of a risk occurring and the severity of its impact. This helps in assigning risk levels and understanding their relative

significance.

5. **Risk Mitigation Strategies**: After assessing risks, the project team develops strategies to mitigate or manage these risks. This may involve contingency plans, risk transfer, risk acceptance, or risk avoidance measures.

6. **Monitoring and Control**: Throughout the project's lifecycle, the identified risks are continuously monitored. If necessary, adjustments are made to mitigation strategies as new information becomes available or the project's circumstances change.

Based on the above components, it is deduced and established that Risk Assessment is meant to update the original project timeline, budget and objective as mentioned earlier, due to changes in the project's originally defined scope, external environment, or overall risk management efforts. This ensures that the risk assessment remains relevant and aligns with the project's evolving circumstances. The quality of data used in both the original and subsequent assessments is crucial, as it directly influences the accuracy of risk assessments and the effectiveness of resulting risk management decisions.

PREVENTING RISKS FROM IMPACTING ORGANIZATIONAL GOALS

Risk Assessment becomes essential to proactively identify, evaluate, and manage potential risks that could impact the project's success. Below are a few examples to vividly demonstrate why risk assessments prove helpful:

1. **Early Risk Identification**: Now, there's a construction company aimed at building a new office complex. In the initial stages, identifying risks like adverse weather conditions, supply chain disruptions, or unforeseen site challenges is vital. Early risk assessment allows the project team to develop contingency plans, ensuring that work progresses smoothly even in the face of unexpected challenges.

2. **Continuous Risk Reassessment**: A software development project provides an excellent example of the need for ongoing risk reassessment. As the project unfolds, new risks may emerge, such as changes in technology trends such as relying on PPC or Bark per se, and then needing to switch to other means because of a drastic fluctuation or downfall in results, or random security vulnerabilities. Regular risk reassessment ensures that the project adapts to evolving circumstances and remains aligned with its objectives.

3. **Tailoring to Project Scope**: The frequency of risk reassessment is influenced by the project's scope and complexity. Larger, more intricate projects may require more frequent assessments, while smaller projects may need fewer. For instance, a multi-year infrastructure project may undergo quarterly risk reassessments to account for changing environmental regulations, while a short-term marketing campaign may only require a single reassessment.

4. Preparedness and Opportunity: Risk assessments put project teams in a state of preparedness. Consider a product launch project. By identifying potential risks such as production delays or marketing challenges, the team can develop strategies to mitigate these risks. Moreover, a well-executed risk assessment can reveal opportunities, like entering new markets or leveraging innovative technologies, that can enhance project outcomes.

5. Managing the Triple Constraints: In project management, the triple constraints of cost, time, and scope are interrelated. A risk assessment directly impacts these constraints. For example, a manufacturing project that fails to assess the risk of raw material shortages may encounter cost overruns and delays due to unexpected supply chain disruptions. Identifying and addressing such risks early can help manage costs, timelines, and quality.

Whether we are concerned with construction, software development, infrastructure, or marketing; risk assessment proves to serve as a vital tool for project teams and managers, enabling them to proactively prevent potential risks from derailing project objectives and goals. By identifying and evaluating common project risks, such as **scope creep**, **low performance**, **high costs**, **time crunches**, **stretched resources**, **operational changes**, and **lack of clarity**, teams can take strategic measures to counter any and every challenge they are faced with.

For instance, through early risk identification, teams can establish clear project parameters, communicate scope effectively, and schedule regular progress check-ins to ward off scope creeps.

Anticipating potential performance risks and promoting open communication among team members can mitigate low performance. Accurate budgeting and regular check-ins help prevent cost overruns.

Moreover, risk assessments encourage teams to overestimate task durations and build in time contingency to address time crunches effectively. Resource allocation plans ensure that there are enough resources to complete the project. Awareness of operational changes allows teams to prepare for transitions, minimizing disruptions. Not to forget, risk assessments combat lack of clarity by ensuring project requirements are well-defined, stakeholders are on the same page, and project information is accessible to all team members.

Real-time Example:

Let's consider a software development project for creating a new mobile application. During the initial risk assessment, the project team identifies a potential risk related to changes in technology trends. The team recognizes that relying solely on a specific pay-per-click (PPC) advertising strategy might become ineffective if there is a sudden fluctuation or downfall in results.

In response to this risk, the team develops a contingency plan that includes regularly reassessing marketing strategies and being adaptable to changes in the advertising landscape. As the project unfolds, the risk assessment proves crucial when a new marketing platform, different from the initially planned PPC approach, emerges as more effective. The team, having continuously reassessed risks, quickly adapts to the evolving circumstances, ensuring the project remains aligned with its objectives and avoids potential setbacks related to marketing effectiveness.

This real-time example illustrates how risk assessment in a software development project can prevent negative impacts on organizational goals by anticipating and proactively addressing changes in technology trends and marketing strategies.

CHAPTER 2
PLANNING AND SCHEDULING

Project planning and scheduling are the dynamic duo that serve as the bedrock of successful project management. These two interconnected processes provide the roadmap, the guiding light, and the structure needed to transform ideas and goals into tangible results. Whether you're embarking on a small-scale initiative or managing a complex, multifaceted project, after effective planning, and scheduling are essential for achieving your objectives efficiently and within the allocated resources.

WHY PROJECT PLANNING AND SCHEDULING IS IMPORTANT?

The important components of effective project management are scheduling and planning. They are the basis of any successful project, guaranteeing its progress and achievement of its goals.

Project planning and scheduling can take the organization's strategic goals into account to make sure the work greatly advances the organization's goals and objectives.

One of the most important aspects of project scheduling and planning is the distribution of resources. To make sure that resources are available when needed, it is necessary to assign staff, supplies, and machinery in an efficient manner. This maximizes the utilization of the resources at hand while cutting down on unnecessary expenses and time.

One of the most important aspects of scheduling is managing project timelines. The project can be broken up into smaller, more manageable jobs, making it possible to closely monitor development and spot problems immediately on. By taking a step-by-step strategy, project managers can keep a tight grip on the project's schedule and guide it in the right direction.

Project planning and scheduling help with managing expenses in addition to time management. They offer a thorough examination of project expenses, which helps to prevent exceeding costs and keep spending under budget. The organization's entire financial stability depends on these financial limitations.

Planning also involves risk management, which is another important aspect. It comprises determining possible risks and uncertainties as well as developing strategies for their management. By planning ahead and establishing a defined timeframe, project managers are able to address risks and minimize the effects they have on the project's success.

Planning allows for the integration of quality assurance within the project. It creates the procedures and quality standards needed for the project and adds them to the timetable. This guarantees that the project's quality is upheld throughout its entire lifecycle, boosting both the project's success and the company's reputation for producing high-quality work.

One of the main advantages of project planning and scheduling is clear communication. These resources offer a thorough project overview, assisting all participants in comprehending the project's scope, objectives, and advancement. To make sure that everyone involved in the project is informed and working toward the same goals, effective communication is crucial.

The transparency that planning and scheduling offer promotes stakeholder engagement. There are frequently many different stakeholders in projects, ranging from clients and team members to government agencies and the general public. Planning and scheduling tools help all stakeholders understand what to expect and when, which improves stakeholder satisfaction.

Planning and scheduling help to increase efficiency. Workflow inefficiencies can be found and removed by segmenting the project into manageable parts. As a result, the project is carried out more effectively, which saves time and money.

Additionally, scheduling aids in determining resource limitations and job interdependence. This guarantees proper job sequencing, preventing bottlenecks, and maximizing resource usage. This in turn helps the project be effective and successful.

Real-time Example:

Consider a construction project for building a new sustainable office building. In the project planning and scheduling phase, the team identifies the need for specific resources, such as eco-friendly materials and specialized machinery, to align with the organization's strategic goal of environmental sustainability.

Resource allocation becomes a critical aspect of the project plan, ensuring that the right materials and machinery are available when needed. By efficiently assigning staff and supplies, the project maximizes resource utilization, promoting sustainability goals while minimizing unnecessary expenses.

Project timelines are carefully managed to break down the construction process into smaller, more manageable tasks. This enables close monitoring of development and immediate identification of any issues. For example, the team may discover a delay in the delivery of sustainable materials and promptly adjust the schedule to avoid cascading delays and keep the project on track.

Financial stability is maintained through meticulous examination of project expenses in the planning phase, preventing cost overruns and ensuring adherence to the budget. The organization's commitment to financial limitations aligns with its overall success.

The project planning process also includes risk management. Anticipating potential risks, such as weather-related delays or supply chain disruptions for eco-friendly materials, allows the team to develop strategies for their mitigation. By addressing risks proactively and establishing a defined timeframe, the project maintains its commitment to sustainability and minimizes the impact of uncertainties.

Quality assurance is integrated into the project plan, specifying procedures and standards for the use of sustainable materials. This ensures the project's quality is upheld, aligning with the company's reputation for producing high-quality, environmentally conscious work.

Clear communication is facilitated through project planning and scheduling tools, providing all stakeholders, including clients, team members, and the public, with a comprehensive overview of the project's scope, objectives, and progress. This transparency enhances stakeholder engagement and satisfaction.

Efficiency is increased by segmenting the construction project into manageable parts, identifying and removing workflow inefficiencies. Proper job sequencing and resource management prevent bottlenecks, allowing for effective and successful project completion. Overall, the construction project exemplifies the importance of project planning and scheduling in achieving organizational goals and delivering a sustainable and high-quality outcome.

PROJECT PLANNING

Project planning is the backbone of effective project management. It's the phase where the entire project takes shape, where goals and objectives are clarified, and where the roadmap for success is established.

A project plan, often referred to as a work plan, serves as a comprehensive guide outlining the goals, objectives, and tasks necessary for your team to successfully complete a specific project. Within this plan, you should incorporate details regarding the project's schedule, scope, deadlines, and deliverables across all phases of the project's lifecycle. However, it's crucial to acknowledge that not all project planning approaches are equally effective. This variance sometimes leads teams to either underutilize or entirely overlook this critical phase.

Project plans set the stage for the entire project. Without one, you're missing an important step in the overall project management process. When you launch into a project without clear goals or objectives, it can lead to disorganized work, frustration, and even scope creep. A well-defined, written project management plan not only offers a foundational direction to all stakeholders but also ensures accountability throughout the project. Moreover, it serves as a confirmation that the necessary resources are in place before the project commences.

To construct a project plan that truly works, a methodical

approach is essential. You must follow a structured series of steps while also being highly specific and clear in presenting your ideas and execution strategy. In doing so, you create a roadmap that ensures your team's success in delivering the project on time and within scope. In this chapter, we will delve into the essential steps of project planning, each of which plays a critical role in ensuring your project's success.

PROJECT SCHEDULING

Project scheduling is a crucial component of project management that involves the creation of a detailed plan outlining the sequence of tasks, their durations, resource allocations, and milestones within a project. This schedule serves as a dynamic tool for project managers to efficiently manage resources, track progress, and ensure that the project is completed within the allocated time frame.

IMPORTANT ASPECTS OF PROJECT PLANNING AND SCHEDULING

To make an organized project management plan, you need a proper structure to keep track of all the different aspects. Regardless of the project type, every plan should include:

Clearly Outline Your Goals and Objectives

You're developing a project plan with a purpose, likely aiming to guide yourself, your team, or your company toward the final goal. But how will you determine if you've successfully reached that goal if you lack a means to measure your progress?

In any effective project plan, it's essential to have a clearly defined desired outcome. Identifying your objectives not only gives your project plan a reason to exist but also ensures that everyone involved shares a common understanding and remains focused on achieving the desired results. Furthermore, research indicates that employees who understand how their work contributes to company goals are twice as motivated. However, only 26% of employees have this clarity because goals are usually set separately from daily tasks. Integrating your goals directly into your work plan creates a real-time connection between your team's efforts and the project's overarching objectives.

Identifying Tasks and Work Breakdown Structure

After gaining a clear grasp of your project's scope, divide it into achievable tasks. Often, this involves using a method called Work Breakdown Structure (WBS). A Work Breakdown Structure is a visual and hierarchical representation of a project that is oriented towards its deliverables. It serves as a valuable tool for project managers, enabling them to systematically dissect the project's scope and gain a clear visualization of all the individual tasks necessary for project completion. Essentially, a WBS simplifies the project into manageable components, making it easier to plan, execute, and track progress.

Work breakdown structure involves the decomposition of major project deliverables into smaller, more manageable components until the deliverables are defined in sufficient detail to support the development of project activities. The importance of WBS is: The WBS is used to plan the project's scope, time, resources, and cost. It helps organize the activities and events of the project. A definite WBS also helps define access and roles in a project. It helps view the cumulative view of project activities. WBS helps create independent and clearly defined tasks.

It is important to ensure that tasks are specific, measurable, attainable, relevant, and time-bound (SMART). Assign roles and responsibilities for each task to team members or stakeholders. This way, it is easier and quicker to attain the desired results.

Allocating Resources

A project's strength lies in its resources. Identify the necessary resources, including people's skills, equipment, materials, and budget. Just as an artist carefully chooses their paints and brushes, ensuring you have the right resources is crucial for crafting your project masterpiece.

Once you've gathered the necessary information, the next step is to assign team members to the various stages of the project. To facilitate this process, we strongly recommend utilizing tools like

Gantt charts or calendars. These visual aids are excellent for illustrating dependencies and connections between tasks, even when dealing with more intricate data such as part-time allocations and tracked hours.

For seamless project scheduling and resource allocation, consider leveraging specialized project scheduling software's. Such software streamlines the process by allowing you to input team members' details, including hourly rates or monthly wages, and generates real-time charts with cost calculations. This feature enables you to compare actual costs with initial estimates, providing valuable insights for timely adjustments and efficient cost management.

In summary, efficient resource allocation and cost tracking are essential components of successful project management, and utilizing advanced tools can greatly enhance your ability to manage these aspects effectively.

Gantt Chart

Gantt charts provide a clear and intuitive way to visualize the timeline and progress of a project, making them a valuable tool for project managers and teams.

It is a versatile tool that plays a vital role in project management. It helps in the scheduling, managing, and monitoring of individual tasks and resources within a project. This chart provides a visual representation of the project's timeline, highlighting both scheduled and completed work throughout a defined period.

By using this chart, project teams can ensure that the project stays on course and adheres to its timeline. Moreover, Gantt charts are considered a standard and universal tool in the engineering and project management communities, fostering unified communication, and understanding among professionals in these fields.

Project Schedule

A project schedule serves as a comprehensive overview of your project, offering a bird's-eye view that encompasses the timeline, project tasks, dependencies, and the team members responsible for each aspect. Essentially, it should be a one-stop source for all essential project information. With a well-structured project schedule that outlines the key details and components of your project, you gain the ability to monitor real-time progress and confirm that your project is on course for successful completion.

This project schedule acts as your roadmap, guiding you through the project's complexities and ensuring that all aspects are carefully coordinated and executed. It serves as a valuable tool for keeping track of tasks, timelines, and responsibilities, ultimately leading you to successful project completion.

Empowering yourself to construct a project schedule with transparent plans, defined processes, and clear responsibilities is vital. It serves as the compass that keeps your team on course, ensuring everyone knows their roles, deadlines, and how all the project components fit together. While creating a robust project schedule may require an initial time investment, it pays off by boosting efficiency, accountability, and clarity - qualities that resonate positively with all involved, particularly your boss who entrusted you with the project. Moreover, it allows you to streamline the use of project management tools, eliminating unnecessary complexities and simplifying the overall process.

Outline your Timeline and Schedule

To achieve your project goals, you and your stakeholders must have a clear understanding of the project's overall timeline and schedule. Having alignment on the time available helps greatly in prioritizing tasks during strategic planning sessions.

However, it's important to note that not all projects come with well-defined timelines. If you're dealing with a large project that has some uncertain dates, consider opting for a project roadmap instead of a detailed project timeline. This approach allows you to establish the sequence of tasks without specifying exact dates.

Once you've addressed the high-level responsibilities, shift your focus towards the finer details. In your work plan template, begin by breaking down the project into tasks to ensure that no aspect of the process is overlooked. Moreover, consider breaking larger tasks into smaller subtasks, making them more manageable and easier to tackle.

Monitoring and Control

As a project progresses, it demands careful supervision, much like a conductor guiding an orchestra. Establish mechanisms and checkpoints to track progress against the project plan. Set key performance indicators (KPIs) and milestones to illuminate the path, enabling you to adjust your efforts when deviations occur.

At the heart of effective monitoring and control lies the establishment of mechanisms and checkpoints. These are the pivotal tools that project managers employ to track progress against the project plan. Think of these mechanisms as the navigational aids that help steer the project in the right direction.

i.**Regular Reporting**: One of the fundamental mechanisms is the generation of regular status reports. These reports provide a snapshot of where the project stands in terms of timelines, budgets, and overall progress. They serve as a compass, indicating whether the project is heading in the desired direction or deviating from the planned course.

ii. **Performance Metrics**: Key performance indicators (KPIs) are essential metrics that project managers use to assess performance against predefined benchmarks. KPIs act as beacons, illuminating the project's performance landscape. When certain indicators fall outside acceptable ranges, they signal that adjustments may be necessary.

iii. **Milestone Tracking**: Setting key milestones is another critical aspect of monitoring and control. Milestones are significant points in the project that mark the completion of key deliverables or phases. They act as guideposts, helping project managers gauge progress and celebrate achievements.

The true power of monitoring and control emerges when deviations from the project plan are detected. Much like a navigator making course corrections to stay on route, project managers use the insights gained from monitoring to make informed decisions and adjustments.

i. **Identifying Variances**: Monitoring allows project managers to identify variances—situations where actual performance differs from what was initially planned. Variances can be positive (ahead of schedule or under budget) or negative (behind schedule or over budget).

ii. **Root Cause Analysis**: When variances occur, it's essential to investigate the root causes. Understanding why deviations happened provides valuable insights for corrective action.

iii. **Corrective Action**: Armed with a deep understanding of project performance, project managers can implement corrective actions. These actions might involve revising the project plan, reallocating resources, or mitigating risks.

Monitoring and control are not isolated events in the project management journey; they are ongoing processes. Project managers continually assess progress, adjust plans as needed, and maintain open communication channels with stakeholders.

Effective monitoring and control promote transparency, reduce the likelihood of unexpected disruptions, and ensure that the project stays aligned with its objectives. In this way, it's much like the role of a conductor who, through careful supervision and adjustments, guides the orchestra to deliver a harmonious performance. Similarly, project managers guide projects toward successful completion through meticulous monitoring and control, ensuring that they hit all the right notes along the way.

CHAPTER 3
RISK MANGEMENT

In today's dynamic and ever-changing business environment, risk management is a core discipline in the field of project management and is an essential component in guaranteeing the successful execution of projects. It centers on the early detection, evaluation, prioritizing, and management of any uncertainties and difficulties that can hamper a project's progress or affect its results.

The capacity to foresee and mitigate risks has evolved into a critical component of project success in a world that is ever more complicated and interconnected. Whether they be infrastructure projects, software development initiatives, marketing campaigns, or building projects, projects are intrinsically vulnerable to a wide range of risks. These uncertainties can take many different shapes, from unanticipated market shifts and legislative changes to resource shortages, technological hiccups, and human-related problems.

Project managers may minimize potential disruptions, eliminate cost overruns, avoid schedule slippages, and guarantee that projects are in line with their goals and meet or exceed stakeholder expectations through rigorous analysis and planning.

UNDERSTANDING PROJECT RISKS IS CRUCIAL

Understanding project hazards is the first step in effective project management. It comprises identifying, assessing, and comprehending the potential risks and challenges that may have an impact on a project's capacity to be completed effectively. To further understand, let's dig into a more in-depth discussion using examples.

In each undertaking, risks can take many various forms and include both internal and external factors. Things like a team lacking project management experience, not providing enough resources, or underestimating the project's complexity can all lead to internal hazards. On the other hand, external risks could be brought on by changes in the economy, new laws, or changes in the market.

For instance, consider a construction project. Internal risks may result from things like a shortage of skilled workers or faulty machinery. External hazards could include unforeseen weather conditions that delay construction or legislative changes that call for modifications to building plans. The project manager can build mitigation techniques by being aware of these hazards. They might do things like maintain backup equipment, cross-train employees, or develop a backup timetable to accommodate for weather-related delays.

IDENTIFYING AND CATEGORIZING RISKS

An essential step in the project risk management process is identifying and classifying hazards. It entails methodically identifying potential hazards and categorizing them in accordance with their nature and consequences. Let's get into a thorough explanation with examples so you can properly grasp the importance of this stage.

Finding risks is similar to highlighting potential project uncertainties. This stage involves aggressively looking for and identifying risks that could have an impact on the project's goals, schedule, or budget.

The critical next stage is categorization, which comes after risk identification. Based on their nature and probable impact, risks are categorized. Technical risks (such as equipment or technological issues), operational risks (such as resource shortages), financial risks (such as budget overruns), or external risks related to market or regulatory changes are a few examples of common categories. Project teams can gain a deeper knowledge of risks' potential repercussions and better customize mitigation tactics by categorizing them.

Imagine about a technology company introducing a new product, for instance. Software compatibility problems could pose a technical risk and cause a release delay. Lack of qualified personnel to respond to client enquiries may be an operational risk. External risks could include abrupt changes in laws that have an impact on the product's compliance, while financial risks might include unanticipated increases in marketing costs. Understanding these risks' characteristics and ranking them in order of importance for mitigation are both made possible by categorizing them. Risks with a high probability and impact frequently demand the most attention and resources.

Project Risk Prioritization

Assessing and ranking of detected risks according to their likelihood and possible impact is a crucial stage in project risk management. Allocating resources and attention to the most important threats requires this procedure. Let's examine a more thorough explanation with examples to better understand the significance of risk prioritizing.

For instance, a high-priority risk in a project to build a hospital infrastructure can be a lack of crucial medical equipment as a result of supply chain disruptions. This risk has a significant impact since it may create delays in patient care and higher project expenses. A regulatory change that involves modifying the project design could be another danger. Although considerable, the likelihood may be less. The project manager can devote resources for finding substitute suppliers and quickly adjusting to any regulatory changes by prioritizing these risks.

Low-priority risks, on the other hand, can include less serious or less likely occurrences, like small schedule delays brought on by inconsequential weather changes or short-term resource shortages that can be handled with current capacity. Although they could still require attention, these lower priority dangers are not as serious as high priority concerns.

Risk prioritization helps project teams focus on the risks that are most important, increasing the likelihood that the project will be successful. The project is protected from significant disruptions and probable failure thanks to this systematic approach, which enables resources, budget, and time to be targeted to addressing the most pressing concerns.

Creating A Risk Management Strategy

A crucial step in project risk management is developing a risk management strategy, which describes how to address identified risks. This plan of action acts as a guide for reducing risks and dealing with them, ensuring that the project stays on track to be completed successfully. Let's explore a more thorough explanation with examples so that you can fully understand the significance of this phase.

The risk management plan needs to take into account a number of different things, such as risk identification, assessment, prioritization, and reaction. It should specify how risks will be monitored, shared with stakeholders, and reported at various stages of the project. This all-encompassing strategy makes sure that risks are actively handled as well as detected and categorized.

A large-scale infrastructure project, for instance, might use periodic site assessments and regular stakeholder meetings to identify risks as part of its risk management approach. Evaluation of the consequences and possibility of probable delays in construction or cost overruns could be included in risk assessment. Classifying high-priority risks, like legal issues with landowners who might object to project operations or regulatory changes that could influence project compliance, is one way to set priorities.

The risk management strategy then specifies certain reaction tactics after these factors have been taken into account. For the infrastructure project, proactive engagement with landowners, impact analyses, and the investigation of alternate routes could be used as legal dispute response techniques. Maintaining open communication with regulatory authorities, remaining informed of anticipated changes, and getting ready for swift adaption are some possible response techniques to regulatory changes.

In order to ensure accountability and proactive risk management, the plan also specifies duties and responsibilities for the project team when it comes to putting these strategies into practice. It describes how frequently risk assessments will be performed and how stakeholders will be informed of the findings. To ensure that risks are not only identified but also actively handled to ensure the project's success, this level of planning and foresight is essential.

Putting Risk Response Strategies into Effect

Implementing risk response strategies is an essential part of project risk management since it entails taking proactive action to carry out the planned countermeasures to risks that have been recognized. The success of a project can be greatly impacted by the way this step is carried out because it is where theory and practice converge. Let's get into a more thorough explanation with examples in order to fully comprehend the significance and usefulness of this phase.

The project team must put these strategic plans into action when risks have been identified, evaluated, and prioritized. Practically speaking, this entails taking steps to either lessen the possibility of a risk materializing or lessen its effects on the project.

Take the case of a software development project when there is a high possibility of a key team member quitting. To provide knowledge redundancy, the response approach may include cross-training team members. In actuality, this entails planning training sessions, capturing procedures, and actively incorporating team members in various project-related activities. This proactive strategy reduces the chance of knowledge loss and ensures that the project will continue to move forward even if a team member leaves.

Another illustration would be a building project that would be at high risk for supply chain disruptions, which could cause the project to be delayed. Diversifying suppliers or keeping a strategic store of essential goods could be part of the reaction plan. In actuality, this entails finding substitute suppliers, building connections with them, and putting in place backup plans like stockpiling supplies. The project team may quickly switch to alternate providers in the event of an interruption, allowing work to proceed without substantial delays.

Implementing risk response techniques requires continual work throughout the course of the project. It is not a one-time occurrence. It entails ongoing assessment of risk factors and the efficiency of mitigation measures. Project teams can considerably lower the possibility and impact of risks by actively implementing these tactics, ensuring that the project stays on schedule and is only little impacted by uncertainty.

IMPORTANCE OF MONITORING AND CONTROLLING PROJECT RISKS

It is impossible to overestimate the significance of managing and monitoring project risks. Since it entails regularly monitoring and controlling identified risks throughout the course of the project, it is an essential stage in project risk management. This proactive oversight makes sure that reaction plans continue to work and that the project stays on track to be completed successfully. Let's get into a more thorough explanation with examples so that you can fully understand the relevance of this phase.

Risks are not static phenomena in the changing world of project management. As the project develops, they could change, manifest, or lose importance. To keep track of these changes and make the appropriate changes to the risk management plan, ongoing monitoring is crucial. For instance, a risk associated with unfavorable weather conditions may materialize in a construction project. The project team can take quick action, such as temporarily pausing outdoor operations to avoid accidents and delays, thanks to real-time monitoring of these conditions.

Monitoring and control also make ensuring that reaction plans are carried out as intended. Monitoring ensures that training sessions are held as planned and that knowledge transfer is efficient, for example, if a response strategy in a software development project calls for cross-training team members to reduce the chance of a key developer leaving. This constant supervision ensures that the risk response tactics are actively used, lowering the likelihood that risks may materialize.

Additionally, monitoring and control encourage openness and communication among project stakeholders. It enables the prompt reporting of risks, as well as the status of those risks and any modifications made to response plans. In a marketing campaign, the project manager can notify stakeholders right away, adjust the marketing strategy, and solicit their input if the danger of a sudden shift in market trends is being watched. This openness and prompt action can avoid major setbacks and preserve stakeholder confidence.

Real-time Example:

Consider a large-scale technology company planning a complex software development project to launch a cutting-edge product. In the risk management phase:

Risk Identification:

Internal Risks: The team identifies potential internal risks such as the lack of expertise among team members in a new programming language and the possibility of a key developer leaving mid-project.

External Risks: External risks include rapid changes in technology trends and potential legal challenges related to intellectual property rights.

Categorizing Risks:

Technical Risks: Risks related to technological trends and the team's unfamiliarity with a new programming language.

Operational Risks: Concerns about the potential departure of a key developer.

External Risks: Legal challenges and market shifts impacting the product's compliance.

Risk Prioritization:

High-Priority Risks: The potential departure of a key developer is identified as high-priority due to its significant impact on project timelines and knowledge continuity.

Medium-Priority Risks: Legal challenges related to compliance and potential technology shifts are considered medium-priority.

Low-Priority Risks: Less likely occurrences, such as short-term resource shortages, are considered low-priority.

Risk Management Strategy:

Mitigation Tactics: Cross-training team members to ensure knowledge redundancy and proactive engagement with legal experts to address compliance challenges.

Contingency Plans: Developing alternative strategies in case of unforeseen technology shifts or legal disputes.

Implementing Risk Response Strategies:

Cross-Training: The team conducts regular training sessions to ensure that team members are proficient in the new programming language, minimizing the impact of a potential key developer leaving.

Legal Engagement: Legal experts are actively involved in anticipating and addressing potential compliance issues, ensuring a proactive approach.

Monitoring and Controlling:

Ongoing Assessment: Continuous monitoring of technology trends and legal landscapes to adapt strategies accordingly.

Training Effectiveness: Regular assessments of cross-training effectiveness and knowledge transfer.

Stakeholder Communication: Prompt communication with stakeholders regarding any modifications to the project plan or potential risks, maintaining transparency and stakeholder confidence.

This real-time example demonstrates how a technology company systematically applies risk management principles to ensure the successful execution of a software development project, considering both internal and external factors that may impact the project's objectives and outcomes.

CHAPTER 4
TEAM LEADERSHIP AND COMMUNICATION

IMPORTANCE OF EFFECTIVE LEADERSHIP IN PROJECT MANAGEMENT

A strong leadership can make any project management successful. Being sure that tasks are being completed on time and achieving all goals are important. Lets talk about the much needed effective leadership in project management and gives examples taken from real-world scenarios to boost our claims.

In project management the effective leaders always start by explaining the project's main aim and demonstrating a big and clear vision for it. By providing it as a road map, the team can be assure that everyone knows the project's goals and direction.

With a strong project management leadership, through a clear vision and goal setting, can motivate people to overcome incredible obstacles and accomplish what originally may appear unachievable. It highlights the effectiveness of visionary leadership in inspiring groups to achieve outstanding results.

BUILDING AND LEADING PROJECT TEAMS

Team Engagement and Motivation: Leadership is about inspiring and encouraging a team to perform at their best, not just about issuing orders. A motivated team is more likely to be dedicated to the task at hand and produce top-notch outcomes. The management style of Elon Musk at SpaceX is a prime illustration of this. Musk is recognized for inspiring scientists and engineers to take on extraordinarily difficult undertakings, like the Falcon 9 rocket. His management style encourages tenacity and inventiveness. His staff is enthralled by the grandiose goals he sets for them, such as lowering the cost of space travel and eventually colonizing Mars, and they are inspired to go beyond what is thought to be feasible. The success of SpaceX has been significantly attributed to Musk's ability to keep his staff motivated and focused on the company's ambitious aims.

Effective Communication: A project is held together by communication. Because they are aware of its crucial role in encouraging teamwork and reducing misconceptions, effective project management executives are excellent communicators. The 2010 rescue of the trapped Chilean miners serves as an uplifting illustration of good communication. In coordinating rescue efforts and updating the public, Chilean President Sebastián Piera and Mining Minister Laurence Golborne demonstrated remarkable communication abilities.

They regularly updated everyone on the situation, from the trapped miners to the rescuers and the general public, so that everyone was aware of the progress and the difficulties. Their open and honest communication not only made the rescue effective, but it also kept everyone united and hopeful in the face of a difficult situation.

Risk management: Successful project managers navigate possible storms just like a ship's captain. They recognize risks, take steps to mitigate them, plan for potential issues, and create backup plans in order to keep the project on schedule. Risk management at its finest can be seen in Captain Chesley "Sully" Sullenberger's command of US Airways Flight 1549's emergency landing in the Hudson River in 2009. Sullenberger had to decide quickly whether to make a safe landing after both engines failed. All 155 lives on board were saved by his cool, calculating leadership, thorough training, and expertise. He had a strategy in place that had been thoroughly tested, and his capacity to carry it out under extreme duress demonstrated the significance of risk management in project leadership. Effective leaders foresee unforeseen events and prepare for them, enabling their teams to handle crises with maturity and competence.

Accountability: Good project management leadership requires holding team members accountable for their work and making sure that deadlines and quality requirements are met. Steve Jobs is a shining example of this leadership quality. At Apple, Jobs was well known for his extraordinarily high standards and responsibility. His management style became the norm throughout the organization, driving Apple to continually produce cutting-edge products of the highest caliber. He was renowned for paying close attention to even the slightest details, making certain that each product matched his high standards. This degree of accountability not only aided in Apple's success but also fostered an excellent culture there.

Adaptability is a crucial leadership quality in a project environment that is always changing. Effective leaders are able to modify their plans as needed. The way in which Jacinda Ardern, the prime minister of New Zealand, handled the COVID-19 epidemic is a powerful example of flexible leadership. She exercised strong leadership in the face of a worldwide disaster by putting stringent controls in place to stop the virus' spread. This method assisted New Zealand in handling the issue successfully. The need of adaptation in leadership, especially during unexpected problems, was highlighted by Ardern's capacity to adapt to fast changing circumstances and make difficult decisions.

Quality Control: In project management, quality control is a crucial component of leadership. Leaders make sure that project results satisfy stakeholder expectations and adhere to specified quality standards. The production method used by Toyota, under the direction of Taiichi Ohno, serves as a superb illustration of this in the automobile sector. Toyota is well known for its steadfast dedication to ongoing improvement and strict quality control. Ohno's visionary leadership was crucial in establishing industry norms and achieving excellence in the automobile sector. The way that Toyota prioritizes quality control is a good example of how leaders may uphold high standards and do excellent work on their initiatives.

Taking Stock of Success: Recognizing and celebrating

accomplishments is important, and effective leaders understand this. This preserves motivation and passion while also boosting team morale. NASA's successful launch of the Mars rover Perseverance under the direction of Thomas Zurbuchen is a notable illustration of this. This amazing achievement was honored all throughout the world, emphasizing how important it is to acknowledge noteworthy achievements. It serves as a reminder that acknowledging and celebrating accomplishments may inspire a sense of pride, purpose, and drive among a team, eventually contributing to the project's success. Zurbuchen's leadership in organizing this challenging mission and the following celebration of its success.

CONFLICT RESOLUTION STRATEGIES:

Resolving disputes is a crucial component of project management. Conflicts can develop as a result of divergent viewpoints, goals, or personalities. Maintaining team cohesiveness and project progress require effective resolution techniques.

Negotiation is a method for resolving disputes that is frequently utilized. This entails identifying a compromise that can be embraced by both parties. For instance, in the business world, two companies that are at odds may negotiate to resolve their differences. The talks between Microsoft and the US Department of Justice in the late 1990s serve as a practical illustration. In the antitrust case, they came to a compromise, averting a drawn-out court battle.

Another effective method for resolving conflicts is mediation. With this approach, a third person who is impartial aids in resolving the issue between the parties. In labor disputes, for instance, a mediator can help employees and management come to an amicable agreement on a contract.

In a more formal process called arbitration, a neutral third party renders a legally-binding judgment in a dispute. For instance, in sports, if players and teams are unable to come to terms on contracts, arbitration may be used. Alex Rodriguez experienced this in Major League Baseball in 2004.

Effective communication is the cornerstone of successful project management, both within and beyond the project team. It guarantees that everyone is in agreement, reduces misconceptions, and informs stakeholders.

The project team must hold regular team meetings. During these meetings, team members can talk about their progress, exchange updates, and handle any problems. Daily "stand-up" meetings in software development provide a practical illustration of how to keep everyone updated on what is being worked on and any concerns that need to be addressed.

Software for project management is also incredibly useful. The ability to discuss tasks, share files, and monitor project progress is made possible by tools like Trello, Asana, or Slack. This is comparable to how a virtual project management board can assist a team of architects in maintaining organization and current knowledge of various design components.

Communication with stakeholders outside of the project team is crucial. Sponsors, clients, and other pertinent stakeholders must be kept up to date on project milestones, modifications, and potential problems. For instance, in the construction industry, it's crucial to meet with clients frequently to provide updates and make sure the project meets their expectations.

Furthermore, reporting must be precise and unambiguous. To interact with superiors or executives, project managers should create comprehensive but comprehensible reports and presentations. Investment managers, for instance, in the financial industry, must communicate complex financial facts in a way that clients can comprehend and use to make wise decisions.

LEADERSHIP FOLLOWS COMMUNICATION

Leadership and communication are like the engine that drive a successful journey in project management. Leading a team involves directing them, establishing clear objectives, and motivating them to produce their best work. It's comparable to a ship's captain using a steady hand to guide the vessel through turbulent seas. Conflicts should be resolved by good leaders to ensure that everyone is cooperating effectively.

But just being a leader is insufficient. The thing that keeps the project going is communication. It's how the group communicates, listens to, and comprehends one another. It's simpler to collaborate and prevent misunderstandings when everyone is on the same page. It is crucial to communicate with other team members, stakeholders, and even when facing difficulties.

To put it another way, communication and leadership are like the crew of a ship working together to ensure the ship achieves its objective. For any project to succeed and run well, they are both necessary.

CHAPTER 5
BUDGETING AND COST CONTROL

IMPORTANCE OF BUDGETING AND COST CONTROL

A key component of project management that is essential to the accomplishment of any project is budgeting. It entails a thorough financial strategy that specifies how costs and resources will be distributed to achieve project goals. The importance of budgeting can be compared to a building's blueprints; it provides an organized method of managing resources and acts as the project's financial foundation.

The ability to allocate resources is one of budgeting's main benefits. It assists project managers in estimating the financial and human resources needed for each job or project phase. Similar to utilizing the proper components in a recipe to create a wonderful dish, this allocation guarantees that resources are used effectively and that the right resources are available when needed.

There is another way to control costs using budgeting. Project managers impose spending caps on projects by creating a budget. This is important because it keeps money from getting wasted and makes efficient cost control possible. It's similar to creating a personal budget where you designate certain sums for entertainment, groceries, and rent so you don't go beyond your means.

Additionally, budgeting is essential to risk management. A well-planned budget takes into consideration all possible risks and uncertainties and leaves room for unforeseen expenses, scope changes, and delays. Similar to having an emergency fund, this safety net will shield you in the event of unanticipated events. You never know when you'll need it.

Notable is also the budget's function in setting priorities. Trade-offs are often necessary due to limited resources. Project managers are forced to choose which features or activities are most important to the project's success when creating a budget. This procedure is comparable to organizing a trip; depending on your budget, you could have to decide between staying in opulent hotels or adding extra activities.

Budgeting also facilitates efficient performance monitoring. Project managers can spot deviations from the budget and, if needed, take corrective action by comparing actual spending to the plan. It's similar to keeping an eye on your bank statement to make sure your expenditures are in line with your budget and that you are financially responsible.

Budgets are also necessary to establish trust among sponsors, clients, and team members, among other project stakeholders. A sense of trust and confidence in the team's abilities and the project management process is fostered when everyone is aware of how resources are managed.

DIFFERENCE BETWEEN BUDGETING AND COST CONTROL:

Two separate but closely related aspects of financial management in a project or organization are budgeting and cost control. Together, they make sure that funds are spent wisely and that project objectives are met while staying within predetermined bounds. They involve distinct procedures and have different functions, though.

The process of keeping an eye on and controlling project expenses to make sure they don't exceed the allocated budget is known as cost control. It entails keeping track of actual spending as it happens and acting appropriately when it departs from the budgeted amount. The goal of cost control is to manage unforeseen expenses and avoid overspending in order to keep the project financially on schedule.

Let's take a construction project as an example. For the purpose of building a house, the project manager has established a budget that accounts for labor, supplies, and permits. Monitoring expenses on frequently is an effective way for keeping project expenses in control. If market fluctuations cause the actual price of items to start exceeding the budget, the project leader may need to find new suppliers, negotiate for cheaper prices, or adjust the project's original blueprint. Managing expenses effectively helps to make sure that the project doesn't go beyond the budget.

However, budgeting refers to the act of creating a detailed budget for a project or company. Budgeting involves figuring out how much money will be needed for various aspects of a project and then spending that money accordingly. The budget is used to make accurate financial options during the project's lifetime. Budgeting sets financial boundaries and provides a framework for efficient resource management.

Using the same construction project as an example once more, the first step is to create a detailed budget that includes estimates for workers, materials, authorizations, and other costs. As a starting point, this budget helps with cost management and planning. It specifies how much each part will cost and when that part must be paid for. It's the backbone that ensures the project's budget stays on track. Effective project management requires both cost control and realistic budgeting. These procedures guarantee effective resource management and a project's financial stability. Let's examine the actual procedures for cost control and budgeting, using examples to help you understand each step.

HOW TO MAKE BUDGETS?

Step 1: **Determine the Goals and Purpose of the Project**

It's critical to comprehend the goals and scope of the project before drafting a budget. What goals do you have in mind, and what are the tasks involved? For instance, you must specify the features, functionality, and overall project goals if you are in charge of managing a software development project.

Step 2: **Calculate Expenses**

Once the project's scope is established, you may begin projecting how much each component will cost. Sort the costs into groups like labor, supplies, machinery, and overhead. Take into account past information, supplier quotations, and professional judgment. In construction, for example, you might budget for labor, materials, equipment rental, and permission fees.

Step 3: **Make an Extensive Budget**

Make a thorough budget that specifies how much money is allotted to each area and when those expenses are anticipated using the cost estimates. This budget acts as the project's financial roadmap. Should your software development project entail recruiting developers, for instance, your budget ought to outline the amount you'll pay for tools, training, and salary at each stage of the project.

Step 4: **Observe and Modify**

Keep a close eye on your real spending in comparison to the budget throughout the project. Check for irregularities and look into the reasons why. Modify the budget as needed to account for any scope modifications or unforeseen costs. This procedure aids in preserving your financial control over the project.

COST MANAGEMENT

Step 1: **Monitor Expenses Frequently**

Begin by keeping track of every project expense as it is incurred. To track actual spending in real time, use spreadsheets or accounting software. Keep track of labor expenditures, material costs, equipment maintenance, and any other project-related expenses, for instance, if you're building a bridge.

Step 2: **Examine Actual and Budgetary Data**

Make regular comparisons between the actual and planned spending. This comparison will draw attention to any differences or overspending. For instance, there would be a cost overrun in the equipment maintenance category if the budget called for $10,000 and you had already spent $12,000 on it.

Step 3: **Look into It and Do Something**

Look into the causes of disparities once they are found. Exist any unforeseen obstacles or alterations to the project's scope? Perhaps the machinery for the bridge project needed greater maintenance because of the severe weather. After determining the cause, take the necessary steps, such as redistributing resources, settling disputes with suppliers, or altering the project schedule

Step 4: **Stakeholder communication**

Inform team members and project sponsors, among other stakeholders, about the project's financial situation. Openness is essential. If the budget has to be changed, describe the reasons behind them and how they will affect the project's scope and schedule. Having effective communication guarantees that all parties are in agreement.

Organizations can make educated judgments, prioritize projects, manage risks, and uphold stakeholder trust when they are able to develop realistic budgets and implement cost management measures. These procedures provide a methodical approach to money management, averting overspending and enabling flexibility in the face of unforeseen difficulties.

In the end, firms that successfully integrate cost control and planning achieve long-term profitability and growth. It's more than just a financial exercise; it's the cornerstone that supports long-term success, effective resource management, and healthy financial health.

Real-time Example:

Project: Software Development for a New Mobile Application

Importance of Budgeting:

Determine Goals and Purpose:

Goal: Develop and launch a feature-rich mobile application.

Tasks: Design, coding, testing, marketing, and launch.

Calculate Expenses:

Categories: Labor (developers, designers), Supplies (software tools, licenses), Marketing (advertising, promotions), Overhead (office space, utilities).

Estimates: Based on historical data, quotes from suppliers, and professional judgment.

Make an Extensive Budget:

Budget Breakdown: Allocating funds for each phase of development and marketing.

Example: Hiring developers, purchasing software licenses, marketing campaigns at different stages.

Observe and Modify:

Monitoring: Regularly comparing actual spending to the budget.

Adjustments: Modify the budget for scope changes, unforeseen costs, or shifts in project requirements.

Cost Management:

Monitor Expenses Frequently:

Tracking: Real-time tracking of expenses using spreadsheets or accounting software.

Examples: Tracking labor costs, software licenses, marketing expenses.

Examine Actual and Budgetary Data:

Comparison: Regularly comparing actual spending to the planned budget.

Example: If the budget allocated $50,000 for marketing and $60,000 was spent, there's a variance.

Look into It and Do Something:

Investigation: Identifying reasons for disparities, e.g., increased marketing costs due to unexpected market trends.

Actions: Adjusting the budget, renegotiating with marketing partners, or re-evaluating marketing strategies.

Stakeholder Communication:

Communication: Informing stakeholders about the financial situation, explaining budget changes, and their impact on the project.

Example: Communicating to the project team and sponsors about increased marketing expenses due to unforeseen market dynamics.

Result:

By integrating budgeting and cost control, the software development project ensures financial stability, avoids overspending, and adapts to unforeseen challenges.

Open communication with stakeholders fosters trust, as they are aware of how resources are managed and any necessary adjustments to the budget.

CHAPTER 6
QUALITY ASSURANCE AND CONTROL

IMPORTANCE OF QUALITY ASSURANCE AND CONTROL

In order to guarantee the quality of goods and services across a range of industries, quality assurance (QA) and quality control (QC) are crucial components. These procedures are essential for upholding strict standards, avoiding errors, and satisfying client demands.

Quality assurance (QA) is a proactive strategy that includes establishing organizational standards, guidelines, and methodical procedures. With an emphasis on the complete production or service delivery cycle, it seeks to avoid quality problems before they arise. Organizations create a framework for continuously achieving or surpassing client expectations by putting quality assurance (QA) into practice. By taking a proactive stance, the possibility of errors is reduced, which eventually increases client happiness and loyalty.

On the other hand, quality control (QC) is a reactive process that focuses on examining, testing, and rating goods and services at various production stages. Finding flaws, inconsistencies, or departures from set quality standards is its main goal. Testing, audits, and inspections are ways that quality control (QC) makes sure that the finished good or service meets the required standards. Quality control serves as a safety net to identify and address problems after they have already happened, avoiding inferior goods or services from being used by clients and possibly harming a business's reputation.

It is impossible to exaggerate the importance of QA and QC. Numerous advantages stem from these procedures, such as enhanced client contentment, financial savings, adherence to regulations, and danger mitigation. Sustaining a high standard of quality for goods or services promotes consumer loyalty, strengthens the company's brand, and helps to establish trust. Through defect prevention and early issue detection, quality assurance and QC help lower rework expenses, warranty claims, and customer complaints. They are especially critical in regulated businesses, where adhering to safety and legal requirements is necessary to prevent negative legal and financial outcomes. Additionally, QA and QC offer insightful data and useful information for ongoing improvement, empowering businesses to better their goods and services and make wise decisions.

QUALITY ASSURANCE AND CONTROL IN VARIOUS SECTORS

In project management, both quality assurance (QA) and quality control (QC) are essential. Every industry has its own special traits, difficulties, and demands, and the application of QA and QC procedures can have a big impact on project outcomes and success. Let's examine in more depth how these processes impact various sectors:

CONSTRUCTION SECTOR

To guarantee that infrastructure projects and structures are enduring, safe, and in compliance with building norms and laws, QA and QC are crucial in the construction sector. Establishing construction standards, project scheduling, and quality management systems are all part of the QA process. During construction, QC involves material testing, on-site inspections, and quality checks. Construction projects can become safer and more productive by lowering the risk of mishaps, delays in project completion, and expensive rework through effective quality assurance and control.

One of the biggest construction management companies in the world, Turner Construction Company, is a prime example of quality control and assurance in the construction industry. Their project managers are in charge of managing big projects including high-rises, stadiums, and hospitals. Turner Construction is a model of quality assurance in construction projects because of their strict commitment to safety regulations, quality checks, and construction code compliance. Project delays and safety issues are reduced by their dedication to quality and safety.

INFORMATION TECHNOLOGY (IT) SECTOR

QA concentrates on designing software development methods, testing methodologies, and quality standards in IT project management. QA consists of bug tracking, testing, and code reviews.

In IT projects, quality assurance and control are essential to producing dependable software products that satisfy user needs. Software projects may experience bugs, security flaws, and performance problems in the absence of certain procedures, which could result in unhappy customers and higher maintenance expenses.

In the IT industry, Google is renowned for its quality control and assurance. At Google, project managers prioritize quality through continuous integration, automated testing, and in-depth code reviews. As an illustration, the Chrome browser project by Google is renowned for its stringent testing procedures, which guarantee a reliable and safe browsing experience. Google establishes an industry standard for dependable and high-performing software products by placing a strong emphasis on quality throughout the software development cycle.

HEALTHCARE INDUSTRY

To guarantee patient safety and provide top-notch medical care, QA and QC procedures are essential. Creating and implementing safety standards, healthcare processes, and regulatory compliance are all part of quality assurance. Clinical exams, audits of patient records, and evaluations of the caliber of medical treatments are all part of quality control. Medical errors can be decreased, patient outcomes can be improved, and healthcare practitioners' reputations can be strengthened through efficient QA and QC.

AEROSPACE AND MILITARY SECTOR

To guarantee the security and dependability of airplanes, spacecraft, and military systems, quality assurance and control (QA/QC) are essential in aerospace and defense projects. Strict design and manufacturing standards, legal compliance, and safety procedures are all part of quality assurance. Comprehensive component and system testing, inspection, and verification are all part of quality control. In this industry, poor quality can have disastrous effects, including dangers to national security and fatalities.

Because of the significant risks involved, quality assurance is crucial in the aircraft industry. For example, a project manager at Boeing was essential to guaranteeing the 787 Dreamliner aircraft's quality and safety. They worked closely with regulatory agencies including the Federal Aviation Administration (FAA) and established strict quality control procedures, including comprehensive testing of systems and components. Boeing led by example in the industry by upholding the highest safety and quality standards, which allowed the Dreamliner fleet to operate profitably and safely.

FOOD INDUSTRY

QA and QC are crucial to product safety and adherence to food laws in the food industry. Plans for food safety, hygienic requirements, and quality control methods are all included in QA. Lab testing, sampling, and inspections are all part of quality control. Good quality assurance and quality control assist shield consumers from foodborne illnesses, product recalls, and legal risks by guaranteeing the safety and quality of food items.

A global leader in the sector, Nestlé places a high priority on quality control in all of its initiatives. Project managers make ensuring that the high quality and safety requirements are met by Nestlé goods. For instance, Nestlé leads the industry in quality control by putting in place procedures like frequent inspections and lab testing to guarantee the integrity and security of their food goods.

PROJECT MANAGERS AND QUALITY ASSURANCE

To ensure quality assurance and control in project management, project managers must adopt a systematic approach that integrates these processes into every stage of the project lifecycle.

Project managers should start by establishing clear quality standards and objectives for the project. These standards serve as the foundation for both QA and QC efforts. For example, in a software development project, the quality standard might include specific performance criteria, security measures, and user interface design principles. These standards provide a benchmark for evaluating project deliverables.

Project managers need to create a Quality Management Plan that outlines how QA and QC will be integrated into the project. The plan should define roles and responsibilities, quality control activities, and quality checkpoints. It might include strategies for risk mitigation and continuous improvement. For instance, in a construction project, the plan would detail safety protocols, material quality checks, and inspection schedules.

QA processes focus on preventing quality issues. Project managers can ensure QA by implementing practices that adhere to established quality standards. For instance, in a healthcare project, a QA process may involve the regular review of medical procedures and staff training to ensure that patient care consistently meets high standards.

QC processes involve inspecting and testing project deliverables to identify and rectify defects. In a manufacturing project, this could entail conducting regular quality checks on products to ensure they meet the specified standards. For example, a car manufacturing project might involve detailed inspections of each vehicle to identify and address any defects before they reach customers.

Project managers should arrange for regular inspections and testing throughout the project. This includes verifying that project deliverables conform to the predefined quality standards. In an IT project, this might involve code reviews, system testing, and user acceptance testing to ensure the software meets functional and performance requirements.

It's crucial to maintain detailed records of QA and QC activities and outcomes. Project managers should monitor progress and document any issues or deviations from quality standards. In a food industry project, this might involve recording temperature and quality control data during food processing to ensure safety and compliance with regulations.

Project managers should use the data and insights gathered through QA and QC to drive continuous improvement. By analyzing trends and identifying the root causes of issues, they can implement corrective and preventive actions. For example, a project manager in the aerospace sector might analyze the results of quality tests to make design and manufacturing process improvements for future projects.

Poject managers should keep stakeholders informed about QA and QC activities and results. This fosters trust and ensures that everyone involved in the project understands the commitment to quality. For instance, in the construction sector, regular updates to the client about safety measures and quality inspections help maintain a positive relationship.

CONCLUSION

In conclusion, the foundations of effective project management across a variety of industries are quality assurance and control. In order to guarantee that the goods, services, and projects under their supervision either meet or surpass specified quality standards and client expectations, project managers are essential. These project managers set the benchmark for excellence in their fields by creating precise quality standards, organizing quality management, putting strict quality assurance procedures into place, and carrying out exhaustive quality control procedures.

Effective quality assurance and control may have a revolutionary effect; real-world examples from the aerospace, automotive, healthcare, IT, construction, and culinary industries demonstrate this. The drive to quality assurance and control reshapes sectors and nurtures innovation.

Project managers have proven in each of these sectors that quality assurance and control are not just foundational ideas but also effective drivers of achievement, security, goodwill, and client pleasure. They set the bar high and encourage others to do the same, raising industry standards and promoting consumer confidence in goods and services.

When seamlessly incorporated into project management, quality assurance and control have the ability to revolutionize not just individual projects but whole sectors, fostering innovation, excellence, and long-term success. These values, as demonstrated by committed project managers, are sources of motivation for those who aim to achieve the greatest possible quality in their own undertakings.

CHAPTER 7
CHANGE MANAGEMENT

THE IMPORTANCE OF CHANGE MANAGEMENT IN PROJECT MANAGEMENT

A necessary component of project management is change. It's similar to how the weather is always changing; it's out of our control but still requires planning. This chapter explores how crucial it is to manage change in the complex world of projects.

Within a project, change can take many different forms, such as scope modifications, unforeseen stakeholder requests, budget adjustments, or unanticipated technical difficulties. If not properly managed, these changes, sometimes referred to as "scope creep," can cause a project to go wrong.

Imagine that you are building a house according to a meticulously designed blueprint. What would happen now if the owner decides that they want a backyard pool? This marks a shift. Disorganization could break out during the entire construction process if management isn't done well.

A single alteration may start a chain reaction. Imagine a line of dominoes, each one standing for a different stage of your project. A single unintentional fall of a domino puts the entire sequence in danger (cue the change!). Handling change is like having a quick defender who can stop a wildfire from starting.

Being inflexible in project management is like trying to swim in concrete shoes. When waves of change hit, flexibility is the ability to float that keeps you from sinking. It is a sign of strength rather than weakness to be receptive to changes, revisions, and adjustments.

A project's stakeholders are its lifeblood. Ignoring their wants and needs is like ignoring the fuel gauge on your automobile; eventually, you'll run out of gas. Managing change well shows stakeholders that you're attentive to their needs and dedicated to meeting them.

If a stakeholder offers feedback on how to better the software's user interface, for instance, take it into consideration. Accept the shift. It can mean the difference between a project that is merely satisfactory and one that is truly successful.

However, note that risk is a friend that frequently accompanies change. But there's no reason to get alarmed. Adapting to change is a dependable defense against unforeseen dangers. In addition to adapting, proactive change management helps you spot possible hazards before they become project monsters.

Imagine arranging an open-air gathering when abruptly black clouds appear above. How about you? With a marquee, you may provide cover from the rain for your guests in case of need. Preparing for and responding to change is comparable to having a project marquee ready to shield your work from unanticipated downpours.

HANDLING CHANGES IN PROJECT SCOPE

Being able to handle changes in the project scope is like learning a new move in the intricate dance of project management. The project scope defines the project's objectives and acts as its bounds. However, unexpected changes do occur occasionally, and managing them well is essential.

Envision organizing an unexpected celebration; you have the guest list, menu, and location all figured out. Someone wants to bring additional friends all of a sudden. It represents a shift in scope. It might cause confusion if not handled correctly. Here, adaptability is essential. It's about having the flexibility to replace a puzzle piece that doesn't fit with an appropriate one.

Effective communication is essential for handling scope

adjustments. All parties concerned, including stakeholders and team members, should be kept informed. It's similar to leading an orchestra in that all players must be playing the same melody. Additionally, documentation is important. Consider it a kind of project journal where you write all modifications, conversations, and decisions related to the plan. This diary explains how modifications to the project's plan affect its overall narrative.

ADAPTING TO UNEXPECTED CHALLENGES IN PROJECT REQUIREMENTS

Unexpected obstacles are like unexpected visitors at a party; although you weren't prepared for them, you must handle them politely when they arise in the course of project management. Project requirements or modifications are frequently one of the biggest obstacles.

In my experience, I usually allot some cushion in my sprints, to accommodate such changes. Having some extra cushion or team velocity available.

KEEPING STAKEHOLDERS INFORMED AND

ENGAGED DURING CHANGES

Successful stakeholder communication is essential to any project's success. Maintaining stakeholder awareness creates the foundation for trust, which is essential to any cooperative endeavor. Sharing information about project progress, obstacles, and successes in a transparent manner builds trust and strengthens bonds with others.

Involving stakeholders in the process also guarantees that expectations are met. Misunderstandings are reduced by outlining project objectives, deadlines, and potential roadblocks clearly. Ensuring that all stakeholders have a shared understanding of the project's direction and expected outcomes is possible upon this alignment.

Stakeholders who are knowledgeable about the project are more inclined to support it and show dedication. Those with a thorough awareness of the project's complexities, whether they be investors, team members, or end users, are better positioned to offer helpful feedback and actively contribute to the project's success.

Transparent communication also aids in reducing opposition to change. Project modifications are frequently necessary, and if stakeholders are not fully informed about the benefits and reasons for the changes, they may oppose them. Clear explanation of the reasoning for modifications helps control expectations and promotes a more receptive mindset toward required adjustments.

Knowledgeable stakeholders are a great resource for fixing problems. Stakeholders with knowledge of the project dynamics can provide insightful comments and ideas during difficulties, fostering more cooperative and successful solutions. The project team's general capacity for problem-solving is improved by this involvement.

Furthermore, minimizing uncertainty is achieved by informing stakeholders. Stakeholders may become anxious and speculate due to a lack of knowledge. By lowering uncertainty that can hinder work, regular updates and open communication help to build a more stable and predictable project environment.

The well-informed stakeholders are more capable of making wise decisions. Decision-makers are empowered to make decisions when they have access to pertinent information, whether they be investors choosing to continue supporting a project or a team member choosing to focus on a particular assignment. The project's overall efficacy and efficiency are increased by this empowerment. With the Starship spacecraft, SpaceX undertook an ambitious mission led by Elon Musk. Unexpected difficulties emerged throughout development, necessitating changes to the project schedule and design. Musk openly shared project updates using a variety of communication platforms, such as social media and speeches in public.

Musk made sure that everyone involved, including investors and the general public, was informed by being transparent about the difficulties, adapting design modifications, and summarizing the overall objectives. In addition to fostering confidence in SpaceX's capacity to overcome challenges, this ongoing interaction demonstrated a dedication to the common goal of furthering space exploration.

This example shows how important it is to communicate openly in order to preserve stakeholder trust, set expectations, and promote a shared understanding of the project's progress. In space exploration, which is a dynamic field where unanticipated obstacles are a given, maintaining stakeholder awareness becomes crucial.

CONCLUSION

In short, effective and regular communication with stakeholders is critical to the successful management of change in project environments. As a result of our investigation, we now know how crucial it is for a project to have informed and involved stakeholders.

Transparent communication has a wide-ranging effect, ranging from fostering trust and setting clear expectations to winning over supporters and reducing resistance.

This approach is important because it helps with problem-solving, promotes continuous development, reduces ambiguity, and improves decision-making. It is a dynamic, multidimensional approach that promotes an informed, cooperative project environment.

CHAPTER 8
EXECUTION AND MONITORING

IMPORTANCE OF EXECUTION

The crucial stage that connects planning and achieving desired outcomes is project plan execution. It's the stage where defined plans and strategies are implemented. The importance of carrying out a project plan is evident in many different industries, as the outcome of a project's execution determines its potential for success.

The world of digital gigantic companies like Apple Inc.

provides an excellent example of the importance of carrying out a project plan. Think about the release of the latest iPhone model. A great deal of planning goes into design concepts, production, software development, marketing strategies, supply chain management, and other areas before the product is released. Still, perfect execution is what will make the iPhone launch truly successful. Apple is a prime example of the critical role that execution plays in a project's success because of its ability to manage thousands of parts, partners, and teams in order to make the launch date while upholding high quality standards.

SpaceX's Falcon rockets are yet another outstanding example. Though complex engineering goes into designing and developing these rockets, the real execution stage is where success is sealed. An incredibly intricate synchronization of technical elements, scheduling, safety procedures, and teamwork is required to launch rockets into space. SpaceX's capacity to carry out these plans with perfection— reusability of rocket parts, punctual launches, and unique space missions—shows how important execution is to accomplishing exceptional successes.

Executing the project plan includes a number of important elements in the context of project management. Allocating resources is one. Consider Tesla as an example. Their ability to successfully execute innovative technologies is just as important to their success in the electric vehicle manufacturing industry as their innovative concept. In order to ensure quality while meeting demand, Tesla was able to manage people and material resources efficiently during the vehicle's production phase. This highlights the significance of carefully carrying out project plans.

There is no doubt that it is essential to manage risks throughout implementation. This is seen by the growth and innovation of Amazon. Their success comes not just from designing an e-commerce platform but also from carrying out plans in the face of uncertainty. Amazon's capacity to adapt to unforeseen circumstances (like the pandemic), maintain service continuity, and even scale up operations in the face of difficulties is a testament to its execution prowess.

Don't forget that cooperation and communication are essential to execution. Cross-functional teamwork is essential to Microsoft's ability to carry out projects like Xbox launches and Windows OS updates. Effective and timely communication guarantees that all parties engaged are in agreement with the project's objectives, which produces positive results.

IMPORTANCE OF MONITORING

In project management, monitoring is like sailing a ship through ever-changing waters; it's about remaining on course by continuously evaluating the project's progress, spotting potential obstacles, and making the required adjustments to make sure it accomplishes its goal. When we consider the function that monitoring plays in real-world situations, such the construction projects that the multinational engineering and construction business Bechtel Corporation takes on, the importance of monitoring becomes clear.

The construction of large-scale infrastructure projects by Bechtel, such as power plants, airports, and extensive transportation networks, is an excellent example of how important monitoring is to project management. Monitoring in these massive projects is more than just keeping an eye on things; it's also about making sure everyone is safe, keeping to schedules and budgets, and handling a lot of different stakeholders and subcontractors.

Take Bechtel's involvement in the London Crossrail project's construction. This was a difficult project that involved constructing a new railway line across London. The project's many aspects, such as managing subcontractors, addressing environmental concerns, acquiring materials, and overcoming engineering obstacles, were all made possible by Bechtel's efficient monitoring systems.

This required real-time modifications to reduce hazards in addition to tracking success. For example, prompt action was needed to anticipate potential delays in tunnel construction caused by unknown ground conditions. Due to Bechtel's monitoring systems, these problems could be quickly resolved, avoiding major delays in the project's schedule.

Similar to this, monitoring has several important uses in

project management. It guarantees that project operations follow the budget and schedule that have been set forth. For example, Google significantly relies on monitoring to track the development process while delivering a new feature or product. Key performance indicators (KPIs) are continuously monitored by their project managers to make sure the project stays on schedule and to enable prompt interventions in the event that deviations arise.

Moreover, monitoring aids risk management by early detection of possible dangers or problems. Updates on Facebook's platform bear this out. While changes are being rolled out, Facebook keeps a close eye on market trends, user comments, and technical issues. By quickly recognizing problems and implementing the required changes before they become worse, this monitoring contributes to a smoother user experience.

Monitoring also helps with resource optimization. Think about a pharmaceutical corporation that develops new drugs, such as Pfizer. Utilizing monitoring technologies, Pfizer's project managers keep tabs on how resources are being used. This helps to maximize drug development efficiency by ensuring that lab resources, research teams, and timeframes are all in sync.

Effective monitoring also promotes accountability and openness. Organizations such as Toyota, renowned for their lean manufacturing methodologies, employ factory floor monitoring systems. These tools make it possible to track production progress in real time, guaranteeing team transparency and holding people responsible for their assigned responsibilities and deadlines.

PERFORMANCE MEASUREMENT AND REPORTING

In project management, performance measurement and reporting act as the project's compass and map, offering insights, analysis, and feedback on its advancement and efficacy in order to steer it toward success. Examining real-world instances where thorough performance measurement and reporting have greatly aided in project success demonstrates the importance of this component.

Think of a business like Coca-Cola, which is well-known for its innovative products and worldwide reach. Performance reporting and measuring are essential whether starting a new beverage line or entering a new market. To assess the effectiveness of their projects, Coca-Cola's project managers regularly monitor a range of performance indicators, including sales numbers, market penetration rates, customer feedback, and production efficiencies. These metrics help in making well-informed decisions, modifying plans, and efficiently allocating resources to guarantee the project's success.

In the same way, IBM and other companies largely rely on performance measurement and reporting when developing and implementing software solutions. IBM's project managers assess the success of their projects using performance measures like software quality, user engagement, and deadline adherence. They can find areas for improvement, streamline procedures, and provide their customers with high-quality products thanks to this data-driven strategy.

While giving it a closer look, reporting and performance monitoring are essential components of risk management. For example, in the automobile sector, businesses such as Toyota regularly monitor and report on several areas of production, such as supply chain disruptions, defect rates, and assembly line efficiency. With the use of this data-driven strategy, Toyota's project managers are able to minimize disruptions that could affect project outcomes by proactively identifying possible hazards, swiftly addressing them, and ensuring smooth operations.

Even the governments rely on performance reporting and monitoring for major projects in the context of infrastructure development.

DATA-DRIVEN DECISION-MAKING MAKING IS CRUCIAL

Throughout the project lifecycle, data-driven decision-making is the foundation for making well-informed, intelligent and practical decisions in project management. This strategy makes use of both quantitative and qualitative data prepare them for decisions, resolve issues, and minimize procedures. In today's complex and competitive corporate environment, where successful initiatives depend on making decisions based on reliable information, the importance of it is significant.

Consider a situation where data-driven decision-making is essential to drug development projects at a pharmaceutical corporation such as Pfizer. Pfizer makes decisions on which drug ideas to move forward in the development pipeline based on a thorough review of research data, clinical trial outcomes, and market analysis. By reducing risks, optimizing resource allocation, and streamlining the drug development process, this data-driven strategy eventually results in the effective introduction of new drugs.

Similar to that, in the technology industry, organizations such as Google heavily rely on data-driven decision-making for project management. Google gathers user data, runs A/B testing, and examines customer comments while creating new features or products in order to enhance and improve their offers. They can make well-informed decisions on feature updates, improving user experience and maintaining market competitiveness, thanks to this data-driven strategy.

Remember that risk management depends heavily on data-driven decision-making. Imagine a building project overseen by a business such as Bechtel. Through the utilization of past project data, geological surveys, and real-time monitoring, the project managers at Bechtel are able to predict future risks such as supply chain disruptions or geological issues. As a result, they can proactively create backup plans and take actions to lessen the effects of these risks, keeping the project moving forward.

Not only this but data-driven decision-making also encourages flexibility and agility. Companies like Amazon rely largely on data to make judgments about inventory management, price tactics, and client preferences in a fast-paced market like e-commerce. Amazon is able to quickly adjust its tactics, maximize its product offers, and meet shifting customer wants by examining real-time sales data and market trends.

The capacity of data-driven decision-making to offer unbiased insights, lower uncertainty, and raise the chance of project success makes it necessary for project management. It gives stakeholders and project managers the ability to make decisions based on facts rather to just intuition or prior knowledge. Better project outcomes are the end result of this strategy, which also reduces risk and improves processes and resource allocation.

Overall, the capacity to properly collect and interpret data is critical for successful project management in today's data-driven world. Examples from the real world, including Pfizer, Google, Bechtel, and Amazon, show how using data to inform decisions not only improves project efficiency but also stimulates innovation and competitiveness across a range of industries.

ADDRESSING ISSUES AND DEVIATIONS PROMPTLY

Promptly addressing problems and deviations in project management is essential to preserving project momentum, guaranteeing goal alignment, and reducing potential risks that might hinder progress. Quick action can have a big impact on project results and save minor issues from becoming bigger ones.

First of all, it's critical to spot problems and deviations early on. By putting in place strong monitoring systems, project managers can identify plan deviations or unforeseen issues early on. This entails tracking KPIs and milestones with project management tools or software, reporting progress, and doing routine status checks.

Analyzing a problem or deviation's underlying cause is crucial once it has been discovered. This might include a careful examination of the events that led to the anomaly or problem. For instance, in software development, unanticipated technical difficulties, budget limitations, or sophisticated coding could all be the cause of a project milestone delay. For a resolution to be effective, it is essential to comprehend what is causing the issue.

After that, rank and categorize the problems according to their importance and urgency. Not every problem affects the project's overall success to the same extent. Determining the priority and possible outcomes aids in determining the sequence in which to handle them. Prioritizing attention should be given to urgent problems that seriously jeopardize the project's schedule or quality.

It is essential to create a proactive action plan. This is coming up with ideas for fixes or different strategies to lessen the problem or deviance. It could include shifting resources around, rearranging deadlines, looking for more help, or changing the scope of the project. For example, in the event that a manufacturing defect is found in a production line, the first course of action could be to stop production, fix the problem, and make sure quality control is in place before continuing.

Timely resolution of challenges requires effective communication. It is essential to keep stakeholders informed about the deviation or problem, its possible effects, and the suggested fixes. Openness promotes trust and facilitates group problem-solving. It is imperative to provide stakeholders with regular updates regarding the resolution of issues in order to sustain their trust in the project.

It is essential that you rapidly implement your chosen solution. The action plan's prompt implementation avoids additional delays or difficulties. To account for the changes, this could involve reallocating resources, updating project timetables, or rearranging responsibilities.

Lastly, it's critical to assess the resolution's effectiveness. Evaluate whether the adopted solution met the project's goals and solved the problem in an efficient manner. The project plans and strategies for the future can be improved by drawing lessons from previous experiences.

CONCLUSION

Effectiveness in project management requires more than just creating a plan; it also requires carrying it out efficiently, keeping an eye on developments in real-time, evaluating performance, making data-driven decisions, and quickly resolving deviations. These interdependent components are what make a project successful. Businesses in a variety of sectors, including technology behemoths like Google and prominent players in the construction sector like Bechtel, stress the importance of these elements in attaining favorable results.

While carrying out the project plan establishes the foundation, performance evaluation and real-time monitoring guarantee that the project remains on course. Using data to inform decisions increases the accuracy of the decisions made and facilitates flexibility and response to changing conditions. As the safety net, promptly addressing problems and deviations keeps small setbacks from completely derailing the project.

The combined effect of these elements shows how well they work together. They promote transparency, improve project resilience, and make proactive course changes possible. When combined, they create a strong framework for project management that not only foresees obstacles but also seizes opportunities, ultimately resulting in the effective completion of the project while reaching or surpassing the predetermined goals and objectives.

CHAPTER 9
PROJECT CLOSURE

IMPORTANCE OF PROJECT CLOSURE

As the last stage of the project lifecycle, project closure is important in determining the project's overall success and the lessons it has taught. From a project management perspective, it is important for a number of reasons.

Validating project objectives against achieved outcomes is one of the main aspects. It's the critical point in the project where the original objectives are carefully weighed against the accomplishments. This assessment serves as a compass for subsequent projects and not only confirms success but also provides priceless insights for future endeavors.

During the closure phase, effective communication—which is frequently the foundation of good project management—is important. It includes presenting a thorough final report, exchanging insights, and acknowledging accomplishments. In addition to strengthening stakeholder connections and fostering a culture of knowledge sharing, this open communication makes it easier for feedback to accumulate, which is necessary for ongoing improvement.

One of the most important things to consider at project

closure is resource optimization. It's the process of releasing and redistributing the material, budget, and human resources that went into the project. By strategically distributing resources, waste is reduced and efficiency is increased, freeing up funds for future projects within the company.

Additionally, the closure phase offers a chance to codify the handover procedure, guaranteeing a perfect transfer of project result to the relevant operational teams or stakeholders. By reducing the possibility of errors or misunderstandings, this step protects the project's legacy and makes it possible for the organization to get the most out of the finished product.

Basically, a well-done project closing not only confirms the project's success but also encourages an organization-wide culture of constant development, effective resource management, and smooth knowledge transfer. It is a critical point in time that offers a forum for introspection, assessment, and long-term planning.

HOW TO HANDLE PROJECTS EFFECTIVELY?

Handling project's success is a crucial step that requires accuracy, clarity, and attention to detail. It includes handing over finished project outputs, documentation, expertise, and responsibilities from the project team to the relevant operational teams or stakeholders inside the company. It is impossible to overestimate the significance of this process; it guarantees consistency, reduces interruptions, and optimizes the value obtained from the finished product.

First and foremost, it is crucial to specify and record project's success rate precisely from the outset. Results that are precise and well-defined provide for a more seamless handover process and can include physical goods, documents, software, reports, and any other outputs decided upon at the beginning of the project.

It becomes increasingly important to construct a formal handover strategy as the project approaches completion. To make sure that nothing is overlooked, this plan outlines the obligations of each stakeholder participating in the handover process. Timelines, milestones, routes for communication, and the paperwork required for a smooth transfer should all be included.

An essential component of the handover process is documentation. Complete and well-structured documentation comprises operating manuals, technical documentation, user guides, and any pertinent training materials in addition to the project results at the end. The receiving team uses this documentation as a reference, which makes it easier for them to comprehend, use, and maintain the outcome.

Effective handovers are based on the transfer of knowledge. Sharing best practices, insights, lessons discovered, and important data gathered over the course of the project are all part of it. Through this transfer, the receiving team is guaranteed to have the skills needed to manage, uphold, and expand upon the project outcomes that have been provided.

Effective project result handover is important for more than just maintaining operational continuity; it also advances the organization's success and reputation. It reduces the danger of discontinuity, avoids redoing, and makes it possible for project results to be quickly incorporated into the organization's procedures. It also promotes a professional, cooperative, and knowledge-sharing culture within the company.

WHY CONDUCTING POST PROJECT EVALUATIONS IS IMPORTANT?

Evaluations at the end of a project are very important for managing projects well and helping a company strive for excellence and continuous improvement. They are self-reflection exercises that look back at the project's path and show ideas, pros, cons, and important lessons learned. These evaluations are very important because they give a big picture of how well the project is doing and how well it meets standards and goals.

Performing these evaluations is important because they provide a complete picture of a project's success. They give businesses a way to compare what they thought would happen with what actually happened. When these reviews look closely at how well the project stuck to deadlines, budgets, quality standards, and stakeholder expectations, they find areas that need more work and confirm the ones that went well.

Post-project reviews are also a good way to keep track of what you've learned from doing a project. There is a lot of information, best practices, and lessons learned during the process in them. This repository becomes a valuable tool that helps people share knowledge and learn better at work. It gives a lot of information that helps people make decisions, guides future project plans, and gives teams the knowledge they've gained from past experiences.

These analyses are much more than just a "what happened?" list, and they are necessary to improve ties between stakeholders. By asking for and taking into account stakeholder feedback, these reviews improve communication, boost trust, and show that an organization is committed to delivering value and growing all the time.

Post-project review methods need careful attention to detail and a broad view of the whole picture. It includes gathering all the information about the project, like reviews of the team, feedback from stakeholders, financial records, and measures of performance. When many data sources are combined, they can be analyzed in a way that shows all the details of the project's path.

Also, working together is very important for the review process. Using different points of view and cross-functional teams during the research phase helps to deepen the insights gained and get a full picture of the project's strengths and weaknesses. The final goal is not only to find weaknesses but also to come up with suggestions and plans for new projects that will work.

WHY CELEBRATING PROJECT SUCCESS MATTERS?

Celebrating project successes is essential to building an achievement, motivational, and united environment inside the company. It goes beyond simple thank-you notes. It is extremely important to recognize teamwork, accomplishments, and the commitment made by groups during the course of a project.

First of all, rejoicing at project accomplishments is a great way to raise spirits. It honors and validates the perseverance, ingenuity, and hard work of team members. A strong work culture is reinforced when accomplishments are recognized and appreciated, as this fosters a sense of pride and success. This acknowledgment not only encourages people to work harder but also develops a sense of loyalty and belonging that strengthens a team's resolve and energy for upcoming projects.

Furthermore, acknowledging accomplishments encourages further development. Organizations encourage successful behaviors and practices by praising accomplishments. For upcoming projects, this reinforcement facilitates the identification and replication of effective tactics, methods, and procedures. It establishes a standard, motivating groups to pursue innovation and quality in their activities.

Celebrating project accomplishments affects more than just the team involved; it affects the entire organization. It demonstrates the company's ability to produce outcomes and cultivates a favorable reputation both inside and beyond the company. The organization's status in the industry, ability to draw in top personnel, and increased stakeholder confidence may all be attributed to this excellent reputation, which will ultimately lead to long-term success and growth.

Additionally, recognizing accomplishments provides a chance for introspection and education. It's important to recognize the elements that led to success in addition to celebrating achievements. Teams are better able to pinpoint opportunities for growth, evaluate successful tactics, and discover strengths thanks to this introspection. It turns becomes a forum for exchanging best practices and lessons discovered, enhancing the organization's pool of knowledge.

Celebration should have to be sincere, prompt, and comprehensive. It could come in a lot of different ways, like awards, public appreciation, team recognition, or even casual get-togethers. Creating a celebration that is in line with the team's beliefs motivates them to even do better and brings gratitude in them.

DOCUMENTING THE LESSONS LEARNED

Documenting the lessons that have been learned from previous projects is a fundamental aspect of our company's dedication to excellence and ongoing development. It's a purposeful attempt to condense priceless ideas, experiences, and knowledge obtained during the project lifetime for the benefit of future undertakings, not just a post-project assessment.

It's simple to forget how important it is to take a moment during a project's hustle and bustle to evaluate what went well and what could have been improved. Still, the seeds of progress are found in this meditation. We find a lot of information by taking the time to carefully examine the project route. We highlight accomplishments, difficulties, best practices, and potential improvement areas that could otherwise be overlooked or neglected.

Documenting lessons learned is really about our development as a team. It's about realizing that every endeavor, no matter how it turns up, offers a chance to learn new things and improve our strategy. It helps us to improve upon our advantages, grow from our mistakes, and adapt our tactics so that we can be stronger and more successful in the future.

Furthermore, our teams use these recorded teachings as a compass. They provide a roadmap for well-informed decision-making, allowing us to foresee probable obstacles, reduce risks, and expedite procedures. It's like taking a deep breath from a well of knowledge that guides our decisions, inspires us to act wisely, and eventually improves the caliber of our output.

Additionally, our organization's practice of documenting lessons learned promotes cooperation and knowledge sharing. It promotes random communication and insight sharing among teams, resulting in a shared learning process. It demonstrates our dedication to benefiting from one another's experiences and using group knowledge to promote ongoing development.

Essentially, documenting the lessons we've learnt from our efforts is a calculation that helps us to improve. It's a dedication to gathering lessons from our past and using them to forge a stronger, more knowledgeable future. Adopting this strategy helps us improve our project management procedures while also fostering an excellence, innovation, and flexibility culture within our company.

CONCLUSION

Project closure is a process that involves much more than simply tying up loose ends; it's the result of careful preparation, committed execution, and critical reflection, which sums up what makes project management effective. We have explored the many facets of the importance of a well-managed project closure during our investigation, including the verification of project success, the smooth transfer of deliverables, post-project assessments, celebrating accomplishments, and the vital task of documenting lessons learned.

The verification of accomplishment in relation to predetermined goals is fundamental to project closing. This is the critical point when we evaluate if our endeavors have been in line with our original goals and gain knowledge that directs our future actions. Transparent project results distribution and effective communication build relationships, promote trust, and open the door for cooperative growth inside the company.

Furthermore, the project's closure is protected and resource usage is maximized through the strategic handover of deliverables, which guarantees a seamless transition of outputs. Post-project assessments act as learning lighthouses, highlighting areas of success and areas that require work. This helps us to foresee hazards, improve our approach over time, and refine our strategy.

Celebrating project success serves as more than just an acknowledgement of accomplishments; it also serves as a spur for teamwork, motivation, and a demonstration of our dedication to quality. It drives our organization's culture of pride, unity, and constant improvement and helps us reach bigger goals.

Finally, the act of documenting lessons learned is what it means to be committed to personal development. It's about sifting through our experiences to extract priceless lessons, improving our procedures, and fostering a culture of collective knowledge that advances us.

CHAPTER 10
EMERGING TRENDS IN PROJECT MANAGEMENT

WHY IS IT IMPORTANT TO STAY UPDATED?

Keeping up with the latest developments in project management is essential for success and goes beyond simply following the newest trends. Similar to most other professions, project management is constantly changing. It's common for new techniques and strategies to take place in business management. Staying up to date guarantees that you'll be able to handle the constant changes.

First and foremost, efficiency is vital. Processes are frequently simplified by new methods, saving time and money. For example, agile approaches have completely changed project management by prioritizing adaptability and repetitive development. Agile teams frequently create products more quickly, are more flexible when faced with change, and have better teamwork.

Project managers are expected to be up to date with clients and stakeholders on the newest methodologies. Consider presenting a project proposal to a client that expressly asks for a project management approach based on Kanban. In such a situation, being ignorant or out of date could result in lost opportunities or credibility.

The organization had trouble meeting deadlines and quickly responding to customer requests since it was using traditional project management techniques. The team leader took the time to get knowledgeable about Lean project management methods after realizing that a change was necessary. By putting Lean principles into practice, they were able to find and cut out inefficient procedures, which significantly shortened project delivery times and increased customer satisfaction.

Moreover, keeping up with trends promotes career advancement. In order to stay popular and competitive in their area, project managers should attend conference courses or pursue certifications. In addition to expanding their skill set, ongoing training raises their status inside the company.

It has to do with creativity. New trends often spark innovation because they encourage trials and challenge new trends. Think about the move to project management solutions with AI capabilities. Using these technologies can lead to increased productivity through predictive analytics, data-driven insights, and mechanization.

AGILE METHODOLOGIES

The disclosure of Agile methodology in project management signifies a radical departure from conventional linear approaches towards a more flexible, customer-focused, and cooperative mode of operation. Agile is a method that prioritizes adaptability, repetitive development, and ongoing improvement rather than just a process. Its significance is from its capacity to deal with the obstacles presented by swiftly evolving business environments and mounting requests for quicker, more agile delivery.

Agile places a strong emphasis on delivering valuable work early and continuously to customers, which is one of its key features. Agile breaks up a project's work into smaller, more manageable chunks, known as repetitions or sprints, rather than waiting until the end to deliver the finished product. Teams that use this iterative method can get regular input from customers and stakeholders, which helps them swiftly adjust to changing requirements and improve the product as necessary.

Agile approaches have a significant impact on project management. First of all, it promotes improved teamwork and communication. Agile promotes frequent communication between team members and a shared accountability and transparency culture. One example of this collaborative approach is the daily stand-up meetings, where team members discuss progress and future obstacles.

Second, Agile gives teams the freedom to welcome change. Modifications made towards the end of the development cycle can be expensive and time-consuming in traditional project management. However, agile views change as a normal part of the process, enabling teams to change course and reorder priorities in response to changing requirements or changes in the market without interfering with the smooth operation of the project as a whole.

The emphasis Agile places on delivering usable product increments at the conclusion of each iteration is another substantial effect. This lowers the possibility of producing a final product that falls short of expectations by allowing stakeholders to see measurable progress, offer input, and make required revisions early in the development cycle.

Agile methods also encourage resilience and adaptation. Unexpected difficulties or changes in needs are commonplace in projects. Teams can swiftly adjust to these changes with the help of agile frameworks like Scrum or Kanban, which guarantees that the project stays on schedule and is in line with the changing needs of stakeholders.

Software development is a prime illustration of Agile's practical use. Traditional project management caused a team developing a mobile app to suffer from missed market opportunities and delayed releases because of inflexible planning that did not allow for evolving user needs. They were able to respond to market demands more quickly and enhance user engagement by releasing smaller, functional updates more regularly after switching to Agile approaches.

MANAGING VIRTUAL AND REMOTE PROJECT TEAMS

Now, let's talk about how the world has evolved. A lot of businesses operate remotely these days. Project management has evolved as a result of the increasing popularity of managing remote and virtual teams. It has a significant impact on how teams work together, communicate, and complete projects. It presents obstacles, but it also presents chances for adaptability, a vast category to hire, and international cooperation.

The change in communication channels is one of the main effects of managing remote teams. To overcome geographical segmentation, virtual teams mainly rely on digital platforms, video conferencing, and collaboration tools. By creating clear channels, setting up meeting times, and creating an atmosphere where team members feel comfortable sharing ideas and updates even when they are physically apart, project managers can guarantee effective communication.

The impact on project management is evident in the requirement for increased autonomy and trust. In contrast to traditional work environments, remote teams frequently work independently and across time zones. Project managers need to stop micromanaging their teams and start giving them clear instructions, trusting them to complete the task at hand. Creating a trusting environment within the team is essential to remote project management success.

Managing virtual teams also necessitates a greater emphasis on goal alignment. Team members may view goals differently, come from different cultural backgrounds, or have different work habits. Maintaining consistency and direction becomes crucial when everyone is working toward the same goals, making sure that the objectives are clear, and checking in on progress on a regular basis.

A company well-known for its remote work culture, GitLab, provides an excellent example of how remote team management affects project success. GitLab employs people all over the world in an entirely remote work environment. Strong communication tools and a strong focus on documentation and transparency are essential given this decentralized structure. To facilitate effective remote work, the organization makes significant investments in collaboration software and makes sure that every procedure is documented. GitLab has been able to grow quickly while keeping high productivity levels thanks to this strategy.

Leadership style needs to change for remote team management to be effective. More than just managing work, it's about encouraging team members who might not physically interact to feel motivated, engaged, and a part of the group. Success in remote project management depends on maintaining a positive atmosphere, providing flexibility, and recognizing and addressing the various needs and working styles of employees.

TECHNOLOGY AND PROJECT MANAGEMENT

Technology has had a revolutionary effect on project management, completely changing the way that projects are organized, carried out, and overseen. Technology has brought in a new era of productivity, teamwork, data-driven decision-making, and expedited project completion.

The advent of project management tools and software is one of the biggest changes brought about by technology. These tools have many different functions, such as resource allocation, task management, scheduling, and reporting. They give project managers the ability to centralize project data, encourage team members to collaborate regardless of location and offer real-time project status updates.

Cloud-based project management solutions have revolutionized the field. They provide accessibility, enabling groups to view project-related data at any time and from any location. This adaptability dissolves geographical barriers to facilitate smooth cooperation between distributed teams and stakeholders.

Data reporting and analytics have a significant impact as well. With the aid of technology, project managers can collect and examine enormous volumes of data, which offers insightful information about the effectiveness of their work, how best to use resources and possible hazards. For example, proactive mitigation strategies can be enabled by predictive analytics by helping to forecast potential deadlines or delays.

Collaboration tools have profoundly changed the way teams collaborate. Communication, file sharing, and task assignment are made easier by platforms such as Slack, Microsoft Teams, or Asana. This encourages real-time collaboration and lessens the need for protracted email threads.

Additionally, new opportunities have been made possible by the incorporation of machine learning (ML) and artificial intelligence (AI) into project management software. Artificial intelligence (AI)-enabled tools can predict possible project outcomes based on multiple scenarios, automate repetitive tasks, and optimize resource allocation based on historical data.

Businesses such as Trello are prime examples of how technology is changing project management. Trello is a well-liked option for teams all over the world because of its simple project management system and friendly interface. Its straightforward but efficient method of task management and teamwork shows how technology can improve team productivity and expedite project workflows.

Though technology has greatly benefited society, there are drawbacks as well. Making decisions can be difficult due to the overwhelming amount of available tools. Furthermore, an excessive dependence on technology may reduce interpersonal communication, which could affect teamwork and creativity.

CHALLENGES AND OPPORTUNITIES

Project management is not only filled with challenges, but also great opportunities. Project managers face a variety of challenges in the dynamic landscape that is being driven by changes in work dynamics, technology breakthroughs, and global shifts.

A major challenge is adjusting to a workforce that is becoming more and more dispersed and remote. While working remotely can be more flexible and provide access to a wider range of talent, it can also present communication, teamwork, and similar project vision challenges. Project managers need to come up with tactics that promote cooperation, establish confidence, and guarantee efficient communication among diverse teams operating in different locations and time zones.

An additional upcoming obstacle is the swift rate of technological advancement. Even though technology has completely changed project management, it can be difficult to stay on top of the constantly changing tools and techniques. Project managers need to make the right decisions about which technologies will actually benefit their teams and projects.

Furthermore, flexibility is required due to the diverse nature of project management. Projects are dealing with more and more uncertainty, whether from unanticipated outside events, shifting markets, or shifting stakeholder expectations. To overcome ambiguity and quickly adjust their strategies, project managers must embrace resilience, ability, and flexibility.

But in the midst of these difficulties, there are amazing opportunities. AI and machine learning have the potential to be used in project management in the future to perform repetitive tasks, forecast project outcomes, and allocate resources as efficiently as possible. Project managers will be able to concentrate on strategic decision-making and innovative problem-solving as a result of this technological integration, which can greatly increase efficiency.

Furthermore, project managers have a chance to incorporate these values into their work as a result of the increased focus on sustainability and moral behavior. Incorporating eco-friendly methods, reducing waste, and guaranteeing social responsibility into projects not only confirms international trends but also enhances the well-being of communities and the environment.

Diversity and inclusivity present yet another fascinating opportunity. Innovation, improved decision-making, and improved team performance can result from embracing diverse viewpoints and creating an inclusive work environment. Prioritizing diversity will enable project managers to access a greater pool of skills and perspectives, ultimately leading to project success.

To sum up, the emergence of remote work and agile methodologies have brought about a transformation in team collaboration and adaptation, underscoring the significance of trust-building and efficient communication in virtual settings. With its tools for efficiency, data-driven decision-making, and global connectivity, technology has completely changed the game. Looking ahead, opportunities in AI, sustainability, and diversity balance out challenges like adjusting to remote work and staying up to date with technological advancements. In the end, project management success depends on adaptability, intelligent use of technology, and fostering a human-centered mindset to motivate innovation and produce significant projects in a constantly changing environment.

CONCLUSION

This book serves as a thorough guide to help readers navigate the whole project management lifecycle. It highlights key ideas and tactics while emphasizing the crucial phases from start to finish.

A project's initiation entails determining its purpose, coordinating it with organizational objectives, and considering stakeholders' interests. Planning and scheduling are essential, with an emphasis on task division, effective resource utilization, and creating schedules that ensure successful completion.

A crucial component that emphasizes the necessity of recognizing, ranking, and proactively managing risks is risk management. Collaborative and effective teams require strong leadership, team energy, and communication techniques.

Project success is dependent upon several factors, including financial viability, cost control, and upholding quality benchmarks throughout the project lifecycle. During transitions, project managers need to be able to adjust to changes, handle unforeseen obstacles, and engage stakeholders.

Effective project execution is ensured by data-driven decision-making, real-time monitoring, and timely issue resolution. The final steps in a well-run project closure are assessments, handoffs, success celebrations, and recording lessons learned for the next projects.

The last section of the book highlights new developments in project management. It highlights how crucial it is to keep up with agile methodologies, manage remote teams, make use of technology, and get ready for opportunities and challenges down the road.

First of all, project management is an energetic and flexible process rather than merely a collection of steps to be followed. From the beginning to the end, every stage offers different chances and challenges. Success requires embracing this energetic nature.

Moving on, remember that the foundation of any successful project is strong leadership and communication. It is imperative to create a culture of open communication, resolve conflicts, and assemble cohesive teams. Being flawless is not the hallmark of great leadership; rather, it is about enabling teams and guiding them through difficulties.

Maintaining flexibility and adaptability in the face of change is also essential. Since most projects don't go exactly as planned, effective project management requires the flexibility to adjust and deal with unforeseen circumstances. Accepting change is an opportunity for innovation rather than a disruption.

Technology also plays a crucial role. Using the appropriate tools and technologies promotes collaboration, expedites procedures, and yields insightful data. But the human factor is still very important. While technology helps, successful outcomes are primarily driven by human creativity, empathy, and decision-making.

Moreover, it is important to be thorough at every stage. Attention to detail is essential for everything from careful planning and resource allocation to strict quality control and ongoing monitoring. Delivering excellence in every way is key to making sure the project meets objectives and goes above and beyond.

Don't forget that the secret to remaining relevant is never-ending learning and adaptation. Project management is a field that is constantly changing. Project managers stay ahead of the curve by embracing new trends, being receptive to novel approaches, and consistently improving their abilities.

The most important lessons are basically about being flexible, communicating well, accepting change, using technology but still appreciating human interaction, being thorough at every stage, and having a dedication to lifelong learning. These aren't merely guidelines; they serve as project managers' beacons, helping them to successfully negotiate challenges, motivate their teams, and complete projects that have a lasting impact in a constantly changing environment. It is suggested that readers put these ideas into practice. This book gives project managers the flexible tools they need to start goals-aligned projects, manage teams well, and adopt new trends. They can successfully navigate complex situations, encourage creativity, and complete projects in a quickly changing environment by putting these insights to use.

REAL TIME EXAMPLES

1. Scenario: Scope Creep

Example: In a website development project, additional features are requested by stakeholders after the initial scope is defined.

Solution: Clearly communicate the impact of new features on timelines and budget. If stakeholders insist, document changes, update the project plan, and get formal approval for adjustments.

2. Scenario: Resource Shortage

Example: A key team member is unexpectedly unavailable due to illness, impacting the project's progress.

Solution: Cross-train team members to handle multiple roles, redistribute tasks, and consider temporary assistance or outsourcing for critical activities to mitigate the impact.

3. Scenario: Unexpected Risks

Example: In a construction project, unforeseen weather conditions cause delays and potential damage.

Solution: Include a weather contingency in the project plan, monitor weather forecasts, and adjust schedules proactively. Create a risk response plan to minimize the impact of unpredictable events.

4. Scenario: Communication Breakdown

Example: Team members are unclear about their roles and responsibilities, leading to confusion.

Solution: Establish a communication plan outlining channels, frequency, and recipients. Regularly conduct team meetings, provide clear documentation, and encourage open communication to ensure everyone is on the same page.

5. Scenario: Budget Overrun

Example: Project expenses exceed the initially approved budget due to unexpected costs.

Solution: Regularly monitor and compare actual expenses to the budget. Identify reasons for overruns, adjust the budget if necessary, and communicate changes transparently to stakeholders.

6. Scenario: Technology Challenges

Example: In a software development project, a chosen technology becomes obsolete, requiring a shift to a new platform.

Solution: Stay updated on technological advancements, conduct regular risk assessments, and have contingency plans for technology changes. Allocate resources for training if a shift is necessary.

7. Scenario: Stakeholder Disagreement

Example: Key stakeholders have conflicting opinions on project priorities, causing delays.

Solution: Facilitate a meeting to understand concerns, find common ground, and if necessary, escalate the issue to higher management for resolution. Clear documentation of decisions can prevent future disputes.

8. Scenario: Inadequate Project Documentation

Example: Critical project information is poorly documented, leading to misunderstandings.

Solution: Emphasize the importance of thorough documentation. Implement a centralized project management system for documentation, conduct regular audits, and provide training on documentation standards to the project team.

TIPS FOR EFFECTIVE PROJECT MANAGEMENT:

Define Clear Objectives:

Clearly outline the project's goals, objectives, and deliverables. Ensure that all stakeholders have a shared understanding of what success looks like.

Create a Detailed Project Plan:

Develop a comprehensive project plan that includes timelines, milestones, tasks, and resource allocations. This plan will serve as a roadmap throughout the project.

Build a Competent Project Team:

Assemble a skilled and diverse team with the right expertise for each project phase. Clearly communicate roles, responsibilities, and expectations to team members.

Effective Communication:

Establish a robust communication plan. Regularly update stakeholders on project progress, risks, and changes. Encourage open communication within the team.

Manage Risks Proactively:

Identify potential risks early in the project. Develop a risk management plan and be proactive in addressing and mitigating risks to avoid project disruptions.

Monitor and Adjust:

Regularly monitor project performance against the plan. If deviations occur, be prepared to adjust. Flexibility is crucial to adapting to changing circumstances.

Use Project Management Tools:

Leverage project management tools and software to

streamline processes, improve collaboration, and track progress. Tools like Gantt charts, Kanban boards, and communication platforms can enhance efficiency.

Set Realistic Timelines:

Establish achievable timelines based on accurate estimations. Be cautious not to overpromise or underestimate the time required for tasks. Consider potential delays and build buffers into your schedule.

Budget Wisely:

Develop a realistic budget that considers all aspects of the project, including unforeseen costs. Regularly track expenditures and adjust the budget as needed.

Encourage Team Collaboration:

Foster a collaborative and positive team environment. Encourage open communication, idea-sharing, and problem-solving within the team.

Prioritize Tasks:

Identify critical tasks and prioritize them. Focus on high-priority activities to ensure that essential project elements are addressed first.

Learn from Past Projects:

Conduct post-project reviews to analyze what went well and areas for improvement. Use insights from previous projects to refine processes and enhance future project management.

Manage Stakeholder Expectations:

Clearly communicate with stakeholders about project progress, changes, and challenges. Manage expectations and keep stakeholders informed to maintain their trust and support.

Celebrate Milestones:

Acknowledge and celebrate project milestones. Recognize the efforts of the team and create a positive atmosphere, boosting morale and motivation.

Continuous Improvement:

Encourage a culture of continuous improvement. Regularly review and refine project management processes to adapt to industry best practices and evolving project requirements.

By implementing these tips, you can enhance your project management approach and increase the likelihood of successful project delivery.

www.ingramcontent.com/pod-product-compliance
Lightning Source LLC
Chambersburg PA
CBHW072313290526
45794CB00002B/646